WAITING FOR THE SHERIFF

Tom Darcy

First published in the United Kingdom in 2015
by Sabien Publications.

ISBN 978-0-9932720-0-4

All events in this book are true. Some names and locations
have been changed in order to protect privacy but some are
also the names of actual people and places.

Cover photography by David Norton www.dndesign.ie
All rights reserved.

For sale at www.waitingforthesheriff.com

Acknowledgements

I would like to thank the following people for their support in bringing this book to fruition. I owe deep gratitude to my friends Brian Reilly and Jerry Beades for their relentless enthusiasm over the past two years, and to my editor Gemma Phelan whose support I can always count on. I am forever grateful to John Smith, my greatest teacher and confidant whom I never met but was blessed to find. It is a privilege to thank my wife and our sons as well as my friend Rocco for their understanding during the terrible years. I would also like to recognise the support given by Mick Daniels, Seán Simons and Audrey Kershaw. Thank you to all those who furnished me with information and aided me in my struggle against injustice, at times risking their own careers and livelihoods. Furthermore, I wish to express my appreciation to all who befriended me over the last few years. Your compassion touched me, especially those who suffered the loss of their homes and a loved one as a result of our corrupt banking system. Finally, I would like to acknowledge my brothers and my mother who are no longer with us.

Contents

	Acknowledgements	iii
Chapter 1	Beginning My Journey	1
Chapter 2	The Road to Hell	21
Chapter 3	The Supreme Court Win	76
Chapter 4	Eviction, Twenty-First Century Irish Style	100
Chapter 5	Stories of Eviction	115
Chapter 6	Here's to My Whistleblowers	138
Chapter 7	The Government Knew Everything	159
	Epilogue	163

Appendices

A	TDs Who Signed the Land and Conveyancing Law Reform Bill aka 'Eviction Bill' 2013	167
B	Bonfire of the Vanities and the Evidence?	176
C	A note to our American Cousins	180
D	Statement to An Garda Síochána	182
E	C1 Mortgage Registration Form	185

1

Beginning My Journey

A rural town on the border of the Republic / Northern Ireland. towards the end of December 2013

'Bang!' A beautiful pink Princess bed is dropped hard on the grass. Followed close behind is its owner, four-year-old Shauna. She tries to catch up but the icy ground under her bare feet prevents her from running as fast as she usually would. 'They took my dollies', this sweet angel whispers as she looks up at me with her deep, watering green eyes. With no time to dress, Shauna stands shivering in her pale pink pyjamas. This winter's morning her four years of life are cast into turmoil; for like her dollies she too is now homeless.

Two hours earlier I had been working in Scotch Hall Shopping Centre in Drogheda surrounded by fortunate mothers and children with childhoods in the making. The atmosphere was contagious as optimism and hope flowed, but such joy was now alien to me seeing that each passing year another Christmas had been lost. A time that was once celebrated was only a reminder of the life that was gone.

The phone rang as I embroidered a Santa sock for an expectant mum who stood radiant; and with a smile that would melt a heart her delicate voice would soon soothe her newborn child. How lucky she was, sheltered from this shameful world that cares nothing for mothers or children, an increasing number of whom are forced into homelessness at this time of year. The voice at the other end of the phone shocked me back to reality.

'Tom, please help me.'

It was a man called Kieran, who sounded desperate and stripped of dignity.

'They're taking my home,' he said. Unlike Christmas movies that depict happiness and heroism, the following story holds a toxic memory for five young children.

Abandoning my Santa sock, Dillon my son stood in as I left for a home in the middle of the countryside. It was my first time across the Border and on stopping for directions soft, friendly accents pointed the way. Travelling between two high grass verges, I soon saw blue lights flashing in the distance. Parking a couple of hundred yards away, I got out and walked towards, the house. On approach, it was like a tornado had emptied its bounty. Furniture was scattered on both sides of the boreen in front of Kieran's home. Police Service Northern Ireland (PSNI) officers stood like centurions with bulletproof vests and automatic weapons in hand.

Among the steel guns, navy uniforms and yellow high-vis jackets a beautiful pink Princess bed had been dropped hard on the grass. It was followed by its owner, a four year old blonde, sweet angel named Shauna, who having had no time to put on socks or shoes stood barefoot on the cold ground.

She looked up at me. 'They took my dollies,' she said as the tears dripped from her face but her little voice was muted by the loud pleas from outside the front door she knew as home. A man was kneeling, begging with hands clasped.

'Please in the name of God don't do this.'

His words filled the quiet country lane as he raised his hands to the sheriff, whose band of heartless thugs were removing all that once created a home.

Devoid of compassion and without thought, they emerged from the door again and again with more worldly goods held tight in their former military hands. With personal items displayed for all to view, smirks grew wider and foreign tongues blazed with conversation. All the while Kieran remained on his knees with his heavily pregnant wife, Catherine, at his side.

'Kieran please get up,' Catherine said over and over, clutching her belly. In full gaze of his children, it was an image that will forever haunt their impressionable minds. The rain fell lightly on Kieran's face, which dripped with tears and rain and was soaked by both. I turned to look back at Shauna. There she was asleep in her Princess bed on the side of the road, dollies retrieved and held tight.

My questions found no answers from this sheriff as to whether or not his paperwork was in order.

'Get out of my way,' he shouted in a staunch Northern accent. The PSNI stood like soldiers in Afghanistan, watching this tale of heartache with emotionless expression.

Friends started to appear, gathering up pieces of furniture and filling open black plastic bags with the family's life. Fifty-two minutes later Kieran's family was displaced. A father, a mother and five children were left on the side of the road days before Christmas. My heart paused as Amie, Kieran's seven-year-old daughter asked me how Santa would know where to deliver her toys.

A wall of belongings was now placed outside a home that was once a shrine to a family's integrity. Items peeked out of rubbish sacks – the razor and shaving cream that would find no mirror or shelf the following day as Kieran tries to start his day from a plastic bag. In what is the new normality of his family's life, his children will be teased and ridiculed by classmates who are merely conveying their parents' opinions that are worded by innocent minds. A mother clings to what instinct demanded, as a van is filled with the last of the plastic bags.

Kieran stood peering through the window of his desecrated home. Clean floors were marked with alien boots and cupboard doors were emptied, as the contents had been spilled out. His children looked to him for the protection he believes he has failed to give, thereby reinforcing his growing self-loathing. With the family home now gone, this husband and father turned to expose his vulnerability for all to see. His children's eyes now joined their father's ocean of tears.

Fake smiles were what left me that evening from a couple who trusted their family's future in the hands of those who could not be trusted. Kieran shook my hand and thanked me for coming. I returned to my car and sat there thinking how cruel and evil some men can be. I observed as the sherriff gave the keys of Kieran's home to the banker who had watched the destruction of a family from the comfort of his new Audi.

Six weeks later as the New Year was in its third week, I received a call from Kieran's brother. His tone was quiet and sad as he told me how Kieran had been found hanging from a tree. His eyes had been pecked by birds and his clothes were soaked in urine. A family picture was found on the ground. Having held it tightly, he would have released it as life left his body, a result of the mental anguish that was suffered in silence by a man who did nothing wrong. All he wanted was to raise his precious children, but his pain was exasperated by ruthless bankers who act devoid of humanity. A lifetime of questions has now started as a wife and mother is widowed and her responsibility doubled, adding to the grief of planning her husband's funeral.

Three days later I walked into the church in that quiet community to see every pew filled. Kieran's coffin was decked in flowers. His wee ones' hands were linked together like steps of stairs and Catherine was in black. Each child read out a prayer. As Shauna walked up to the altar she reached out to Kieran's coffin. 'I miss you, Daddy', she said. I instantly joined every person present and wept.

An hour later I stood as Kieran was laid to rest. Forever haunting is the image at Kieran's graveside where innocents gathered to give their final farewell to a father they love. Their little hands held red roses as each took their turn to place their own flower on their Daddy's coffin. The silence of the graveyard was interrupted only by their quiet sobs. Catherine stood holding two roses while she gazed at Kieran's coffin. He was her lover, her best friend, her world, the father of her children and the man she still loves, though now with a broken heart. Tears dripped slowly from her face as she kissed the first rose and placed it softly on the coffin, then raising the second to her lips she kissed it gently and rubbed it across her belly. The last rose to be placed on Kieran's coffin was from the child he would never get to hold.

As I shook Catherine's hand, conveying words of sympathy she was no doubt too numb to hear, I looked at each small angelic face beside her and thought of their life going forward. No father, no home, a lifetime of questions, why? Then I thought of the criminal bankers and all those complicit in Kieran's forced suicide, hoping some day they would see the evil they caused and the thousands of lives they destroy; their crimes now paid for by innocent children and unborn babies.

It was these events at the end of December 2013 that provided the catalyst to my ongoing involvement in supporting people who face eviction in Ireland. I could relate to their desperation and fear, for my family had also faced down the sheriff. The following is my own story and how my personal involvement with thousands of people facing homelessness has led me to unearth the truth behind the alliance between the

Irish Government, the banks and the judiciary and their attempt to reintroduce eviction into Ireland.

My story. Newly married in 1981, I delivered coal around Dublin only for the introduction of a smokeless zone to force me out of business. With a young family to support and little formal education there were few options available, so I became a taxi driver. Some years later, the opportunity to establish the National Taxi Drivers Union of Ireland offered me an alternative source of employment and new way of life. However, due to internal conflicts within the taxi business itself, followed by deregulation in 2000, I again found myself with no income or pension.

Instead of looking forward to the comfort of our middle years, my wife Clare and I had to establish new careers. We agreed that I would support the family and she would realise her ambition to qualify as an interior designer in an area where she had already shown flare and creative ability. Once employed, the roles would be reversed and I would go to university to study law with the intention of becoming a solicitor.

As Clare began her first college term, I started work on building sites throughout Dublin, where regularly assaulted by the weather I became strangely nostalgic for my years behind the wheel. Soon, foreign workers arriving from the Balkan States afforded me the opportunity to move into a management role where, not unlike my taxi days, much of the week was spent defusing potentially volatile situations. With Romanians pitted against Moldovans, Lithuanians arguing with Ukrainians and Croatians refusing to work with Bosnians, my job description read more like a mediator than a builder.

Vergil, a Romanian worker, arrived on the site one rainy morning. A qualified engineer back home, he now collected bricks by hand and cleaned up after his former enemies. Mid-forties and small in stature, his hands were scarred from handling gazelles at Ceaușescu's Palace. Always polite, he would tell horrific stories about the kidnapping and selling of local children into prostitution by men from bordering Moldovan towns, and how elderly people regularly froze to death during the winter months. It came as no surprise then that Ireland was like a new world to him, as was his small bedsit on the North Circular Road. In Romania he had lived with his wife, a nurse, and four children on a set wage equivalent to €20 per month in a town with no electricity. Now he sent home as much of his wages as he could afford, even walking to work to save the bus fare.

As the months went by suppliers and their contact details passed through the site. Creating a rapport with sales agents, I discovered where to find the best deals on materials. Watching the men applying their trade, I also learned about the skill of building itself so that by 2002 I was confident enough to take on the construction of a small extension for a local woman. Using the workers and architects from the site in the evenings and at weekends, the building was complete in under two months.

By early 2003 Clare had qualified as a designer; an unforgettable day as she accepted her degree in University College Dublin (UCD), the first in her family to achieve such an honour. Ill health along with 4 a.m. finishes followed by early rises had not dampened her ambition. Whenever possible, we would read over her work, which gave an insight into design and building construction from a different perspective. Watching her on graduation day, I felt so proud and looked forward to my own turn next. Little did we both realise how everything was about to change, and that my own aspirations would have to be put on indefinite hold.

It all began some weeks later when a planning application notice was placed on the wall adjacent to our home: Belgrove Football Club grounds had been sold to a local property developer. Assuming that planning was being sought for houses similar to our own, we ignored it at first. However, upon further enquiry, it appeared that a block of six apartments was to be built, so, with the prospect of our back garden being turned into a fishbowl, we decided to sell up. As the orange 'for sale' sign was firmly erected, we felt that we were righting the evils of my past within the National Taxi Drivers Union of Ireland and rekindling our life together. In less than four weeks, our Clontarf home was sold and we moved into rented accommodation.

Driving away from our home for the last time, I stared up at the stained-glass windows and remembered the night the taxi mafia had petrol-bombed our home, and how my crusade for the rights of others had wrecked our lives. I also reminisced about our first day arriving into this new housing estate and hoped that life could be as good as that day again.

By mid-2003, with three building extensions on the go, I noticed a site for sale in a quiet cul-de-sac in Howth. Climbing over the wall and walking around, Woodview felt like home, but according to the auctioneer certain problems had been identified, namely that the site had originally consisted of two semi-detached houses until the renovation of one had brought down the other. After lengthy litigation, the site was split and the demolished house was rebuilt on the new separate site. However, an issue with the freehold had arisen, leaving the remaining site without the prospect of a buyer – as a result of which the asking price was 70% below the current market value.

Believing these issues could be resolved, I excitedly brought Clare out to see the site, which she immediately fell in love with. The direction of the sun was noted and how it would illuminate the rooms, as well as how water features could be used to similar effect. For the first time in almost a decade Clare seemed happy, and for that reason Woodview would be right for all of us.

A few weeks later, I was in the Property Registration Authority office in Henrietta Street investigating the freehold issue. Trawling through land registry books from the turn of the century, it appeared that different people had held the title of freehold as far back as the Earl of Howth. Finally, I discovered that New Ireland Assurance had purchased most of the freeholds around Howth in the late 1960s. Travelling to London in search of these documents – that had been drafted during my grandfather's generation – and after hundreds of hours of investigation, I found the owner of the freehold. Not wanting to inform him of the true value of the dusty old files held in a safe of similar vintage, I concocted a story about setting up a leasehold agency for which I needed to purchase freeholds.

'Where are you interested in?' the young man called Jeremy asked.

Guiding the conversation round to the area of Howth, I mentioned that my grandfather had driven trams in the area, at which point he went to his cabinet and chose a number of files. Flicking through the bundles, he removed one entitled Woodview, Grey's Lane. It was like divine intervention. Attempting to conceal my excitement, I asked how much it would cost, referring to my 'business partner' who still remained to be convinced of this venture.

'I'll let you have these for €75,000,' Jeremy replied, holding five bundles in his hands.

My heart sank.

'Tell you what, I'll give you €15,000 for say, this one.'

Appearing to randomly choose the file next to Woodview, I then changed my mind and removed the file I wanted.

'I will buy this one and show my partner,' I said. 'Would you like cash or bank draft?' Jeremy smiled. 'You get the cash and I will draft the necessary.'

Running down the stairs, I found the nearest Bank of Ireland and got the money. On my return, Jeremy was standing with the bundle of deeds in his hand. Counting out the cash on the table, I examined the deeds and signed the bill of sale. Now that I owned the freehold the value would increase by €800,000. Although feeling a tinge of guilt, the stress and difficulties that my family had gone through over the years erased such thoughts immediately.

Weeks later we bought Woodview. Although our friends believed that Clare and I were mad to purchase a property with so many problems attached to it, we were nonetheless looking forward to our new beginning. Such was our excitement that we even ignored the comments of our new neighbour, Pat who, unaware of my ownership of the freehold, confided in us that he himself had considered buying it, but such were the contentious issues that on investigation he had dismissed it as an act of lunacy. As soon as the sold sign went up, in what had become a tradition, Clare and I cracked open a bottle of sparkling wine at the gate.

By mid-2005 our new home was complete save for the interior and the gardens. With glass atriums to the front and the back and a mezzanine over a hot tub with large glass panels that allowed its occupants to view the night sky, it was referred to by neighbours as the Glass House. The front area also overlooked the sea and included a metal, spiral staircase that had originated from the decommissioned Maze Prison; the story was that Bobby Sands had walked the same stairs daily.

Such was the interest in our new home that Clare and I started a new business: Concept Homes. However, first of all I needed to lease a van, but within twenty-four hours every finance company I approached had turned me down, citing my credit history from the taxi industry as the reason. Undeterred, the following day I went into the Allied Irish Bank (AIB) branch in Sutton to make a loan application. Not being a customer, I was doubtful of my prospects and yet while sitting on the new, leather couch filling out forms, I was approached by the assistant manager with an outstretched hand who identified himself as Gordon.

'And you are, Tom?' he asked.

Surprised that he had taken the time to enquire about me at reception, I followed him into his office. In his early thirties and casually dressed, it appeared that Gordon had discarded the old regime of stuffed shirts and accountant mentality to show the new face of banking. Within minutes, like a proud father, I was showing him pictures of my new home and then went on to share my dreams of building designer houses in the same area.

Looking back, I now realise that Gordon's interest in my ideas was as sincere as his new banker's mentality. Sizing me up for the biggest fall of my life, I believe that my fate was sealed that morning.

'Tom, I think we could get you €4.5 million to start,' he said.

Shocked, I laughed nervously. To this day I cannot remember the small talk that ensued between us, but upon leaving Gordon's office all I could think of was putting together projection figures for the build of two designer homes and costs for sites, an exercise I had done many times while driving through affluent areas in Dublin.

Two days later, Clare and I opened an account with AIB using only a gas and electricity bill as identification.

'It's a no-brainer,' Gordon reassured us. 'You buy and build them. It's as safe as houses. Here's a temporary chequebook to get you started.' Taking the chequebook from him, it appeared that he was right, considering that AIB only sought two conditions, which were refinance and full payment, both of which were in its control. AIB was required to issue the finance to complete the development and all I had to do was finish on budget. Gordon was right, it was a no-brainer.

Upon enquiring as to whether or not I could put down a deposit on two sites, I was assured that the overdraft was for €150,000. 'But don't worry if you go over that,' replied Gordon, 'say quarter of a million will be covered.' Trying to remain composed and with not one document signed or guarantee given, Clare and I walked down the main road in Sutton Cross. With the reality of the chequebook in my clutched fist, we knew that this was not a dream. Clare was the first to break the silence as we crossed the road:

'Is this for real or did he just give you a quarter of a million euro?'

Still dazed, I dropped Clare home and drove to Malahide, where I had seen a new development two weeks earlier with signage advertising three-acre sites beside Malahide Castle. Phoning the agent, we arranged to meet an hour later. Doubtful that my old van would instil much confidence, I borrowed a Mercedes from my friend, Paddy, whom I had known from my taxi days and who now ran a chauffeuring company. By lunchtime I was standing on site 21 Myra Manor with Frank Mahoney from Gunne Residential.

'Great sites,' he nodded, 'they have gone up by €130,000 in the last three weeks. I have three left: 17, 24 and this site, number 21'.

Both 17 and 21 were corner sites and had great potential for other properties.

'How much for 21 and 17?' I asked.

'€1.5 million.'

I momentarily froze with disbelief. Two weeks earlier I had been looking out the window of my 1995 Nissan van unable to get finance for an upgrade, and now I was on the verge of buying two sites. Trying to haggle, I offered €1.3 million.

'Sorry, Tom, there's no wiggle room here. These are like hot cakes. The seller won't take a penny less than €750,000 per site.'

I shook his hand and said, 'No, too steep, there has to be some reduction for two.'

But he assured me that they would be snapped up by the end of the week. 'I got these sites two months ago and sold twenty in five weeks. I've being selling property in Malahide for twenty-two years and have never seen anything like this. It's bedlam.'

Sensing me weighing it up, Frank handed me his card.

'Ring if you change your mind,' he said. But he did not need to wait long, as by the time I reached the main entrance I had already done so, especially upon hearing the occupants of the two jeeps parked at the security portakabin enquiring about the same sites.

The figures I had given to the bank were for €1 million per site, which included stamp duty and legal fees as well as a contingency fund of €50,000. So buying them would cost €2 million and building them would cost another €2 million together with planning fees and interest at €500,000. Given that they would be selling for €3 million each and were increasing by the week that would be a minimum of €1.5 million profit. It certainly appeared that Gordon was right: it was as safe as houses.

Making a U-turn, I caught Frank getting into his car. Lowering my window, I pulled up beside him and reached out my hand.

'€1.45 million and you have a deal,' I said.

Noticing the two jeeps approaching, I produced the chequebook.

'I'll give you a booking deposit. How much do you want?'

'Make it for €100,000. That will keep the seller happy,' he replied.

My heart raced as I handed him the cheque, at which point I saw two men alight from their jeep and approach Frank.

'Lads, if you're looking for a site, there's only one left. This man has bought two just now and will probably buy the last one by tomorrow.'

Frank reached out his hand and congratulated me loudly.

Emotions never before experienced filled my heart and mind on the drive back to Paddy's garage to return his Mercedes. Climbing into my old Nissan van, I knew that things had changed forever because now I could achieve all I had ever dreamt of. The thirty-minute journey felt like seconds, and as I opened the gate to our home and saw Clare talking to our sons Dillon and Greg, for the first time in years I felt proud of myself and what I was about to achieve.

Sabien, my Saint Bernard dog, jumped up and licked my face. Following me into the kitchen where Clare was standing, I could not stop smiling. I told her that I had bought the two sites in Malahide. Remembering the years struggling and working hard, with Clare studying until 4 a.m. and then travelling to Dún Laoghaire for a 9 a.m. start, at that moment it all seemed to have been worth it.

Three weeks later, as Clare dressed the Christmas tree for the first time in our new home in Howth, the doorbell rang. It was Gordon who could be seen smiling on the intercom screen.

'It's your friendly banker,' he said, accompanied by a man similarly dressed. I pressed the button to release the gates and greeted them at the front door.

'We've come to see your house,' smiled Gordon, and he introduced his companion as Charles who was another banker.

'It's fast becoming an architectural attraction around here,' I replied, bemused at the enthusiasm of my unexpected visitors. Offering a tour of my home, their compliments about the quality and design of the building were acknowledged, and after mutually extended seasonal greetings and more handshakes they left.

Curious but unalarmed, I was sitting down to dinner when the phone rang.

'Is that Tom?' asked an unidentified voice at the other end.

'Yes,' I replied. 'Who's this?'

'It's Jimmy from the site next to you in Malahide.'

Not knowing him or how he had got my number, I paused. 'What can I do for you, Jimmy?'

'Frank, the auctioneer from Gunne Residential gave me your number. I've just started building next to you and wondered if I could leave my containers on your site until you start building.' Given that it was common practice for builders to support each other, whether it be with a loan of machinery or space, I thought nothing more of it.

'Okay, then,' I answered. 'Work away.'

Passing the site the following week, I noticed that Jimmy had settled his two containers and machinery. The white ropes that had marked out the perimeter on the site were now in a pile of rubbish, but since it would be months before work would commence, it didn't cost me a thought. Little did I realise that this man would go on to use my neighbourly gesture to initiate my and my family's descent into bankruptcy and destitution.

By the third week of January 2006, my overdraft had grown to €280,000. Still without signed documentation from the bank, and with the architects and surveyors drawing up the plans as well as sending invoices, Clare and I went to meet Gordon. Straight out of his office, he greeted us as if we were lifelong friends.

'I have a facility form here,' he said. 'It's just standard stuff.' He pointed to the yellow Post-it note placed for Clare to sign on the back page of a folded document, and then changed the subject to the price of houses.

'You paid how much for the two sites, Tom?' Gordon asked.

'€1.45 million,' I answered. 'With stamp duty, legal and build costs being another €3 million.'

'God, Tom, you're going to make a fortune. They're selling for €3.5 million right now.'

At which point the calculator was produced. 'That's about €7 million in today's market, less borrowings of €4.5 million including interest of €500,000. That's €2.5 million before tax. You could buy a corporate box in Manchester United for that!'

Following more brief small talk, Clare and I returned home where the reality of our meeting sank in. For a moment we were teenagers again, and as we squeezed each other with excitement, the faint emotion from another life ignited once more.

'€2.5 million,' I repeated. 'To think that less than four months ago I couldn't get finance for a van.'

The following week we sat in my solicitor's office where more Post-its were lined up indicating where Clare should sign. By this time almost €500,000 had been paid out without any paperwork. The next couple of months were filled with meetings with architects and planning officers in Fingal County Council.

We were aware that our home Woodview included nine inches of glass higher than planning permission allowed, so we had made an application for retention. Standard procedure for the most part, it would have been a straightforward process had it not been for the neighbourhood planning conservationists who, every Thursday evening, could be seen walking the roads of Howth in search of planning applications. With clipboards in hand they would copy down key sentences from signage erected in front gardens and meet later in the Summit Inn pub to discuss their findings.

From the outset my neighbour had shown an unhealthy interest in our home. Aware that a certain amount of resentment might be inevitable, due to the fact that he had been unable to purchase Woodview himself, I had kept my distance. On numerous occasions, however, I caught him taking photographs and documenting cars and vans arriving on-site. It was only when passing his house soon after that I saw the true extent of his obsession. The walls of his front room were covered with photos of my workmen together with lists of vehicles and their registration numbers written on posters on the wall. At first assuming him to be bored or delusional, I now questioned his motives for collecting apparently innocuous information about the activities at my property. Then, one evening, upon returning late to check work that had been carried out that day, I found the same neighbour sitting on the top scaffolding holding an outstretched measuring tape.

'What are you doing?' I shouted up.

'Just checking,' he replied. Unwilling to enter into an argument, I let it go.

In hindsight, perhaps a more assertive approach would have put an end to this growing obsession, which was no doubt behind the unannounced arrival of Fingal County Council enforcement officers a couple of weeks later. Although citing numerous complaints that had been made about my development it was nonetheless comforting to learn that similar visits had been made to other sites. It appeared that the Howth vigilante planning mob were taking their self-appointed responsibilities very seriously.

During one particular inspection from the Fingal County Council Building Enforcement Section, a man in his forties introduced himself as Derek, alongside his colleague, Mary Goggins – a thin, dark-haired woman, at whom my dogs uncharacteristically snarled; she asked extensive questions about our home and my own profession as a developer. After some time both left, though not without a parting reference to my application for retention – that should it be denied, our home would have to be knocked down. Given that retention was still in the process, this verdict appeared presumptuous, although in light of the events that were to unfold between myself and Mary Goggins, her prediction about the planning process of my home shouldn't have surprised me for her personal involvement in the planning corruption at Fingal County Council went far deeper than I could have imagined.

After a number of months, full planning permission was granted for 21 Myra Manor in Malahide. I contacted Jimmy next door and he moved his containers and we erected temporary fencing. Two of my sons, Dillon and Carl, arrived on-site each morning and we worked side by side. Around the same time, a site recently rezoned for unrestricted residential use came on the market. Overlooking Dublin Bay, the view of Howth Head was majestic. Mentioning it to Gordon, we discussed the possibility of building Ireland's first designer village. Within twenty-four hours, I had €10 million to spend on Waterside in Howth. However, my excitement was soon overshadowed by the refusal of retention for the nine inches of glass to our home that had just been issued by Fingal

County Council, who were now seeking to have our entire home demolished.

Walking into the High Court, Clare and I found ourselves in the glare of the media, and by November, Judge Jacqueline Linnane had ruled in favour of Fingal County Council. 'Designer couple ordered to demolish home or go to prison', the headlines read. Luckily having drafted plans that would sort out the height problem, our engineer ensured that the property remained intact. On a positive note, the hype created over our home brought national attention to our designer village.

Given the issues surrounding our family home in Howth and the possibility of a prejudiced outcome when submitting a planning application for the new Waterside development, we decided to apply for planning in Clare's maiden name. The planner was Aaron Jacobs, and he directed me through the complexities of dealing with the conservationists in the Howth area, which resulted in two separate planning applications required to satisfy potential objections. Finally, in May 2008, for the third and last application, additional information was sought, such as photomontages that would show no interruption to the views. Days later, on 30 May, I handed over the pictures.

'That's all I need,' Aaron Jacobs said. 'You should have planning in a week or so.'

With my heart beating out of my chest, I skipped out the door. A few days later, in what had become my daily ritual, I logged onto the Fingal County Council website and there it was: Planning Permission Granted. Immediately printing it off, I noted the conditions attached. I had done it. The next few hours were some of the happiest in my life.

Sitting down to dinner with my family at 5.30 p.m., the phone rang. Tempted to let it go to voicemail, I nonetheless answered. Maybe if I had let it go, I would have enjoyed another hour with my family, for as a result of that phone call we would rarely experience a happy moment again together. Rather, we were about to be thrust headlong into the centre of planning corruption in Ireland, and in so being, we were set on the road to hell.

2

The Road to Hell

The unfamiliar voice at the other end of the phone spoke with a refined accent. 'Hello, am I speaking to Tom?'

'Yes,' I replied.

'I work in Fingal Planning Office, and your planning is being pulled.'

A coldness came over me.

'You still there?' he continued.

'Why are you telling me this?' I asked in disbelief.

'Because it sickens me what goes on here, and you seem like a nice couple. They discovered that your wife's maiden name is Palmer, and there was a massive blowout with Aaron Jacobs storming out of his office.'

My mystery caller continued. 'I heard him say "I'm not doing that." Then they called in someone you already know, Mary Goggins, and appointed her temporary senior planner, just like that, a position that wasn't advertised or even existed.'

He paused. 'There's no position here in Fingal for a temporary senior planner. In fact we're seeking voluntary redundancies. Anyway, you should check with HR in Fingal first thing Monday morning and get it in writing that there is no position for a temporary senior planner, nor are they advertising such a post. Do the same with FÁS, and contact the Irish Planning Institute.' Then my caller rang off.

21

I sat motionless with the sensation of the mobile phone burning my ear. For over a decade the media had been covering the Mahon Tribunal, Frank Dunlop and the part played by many others in what had been endemic corruption within the planning authorities throughout Ireland. Sitting on the stairs with my face buried in my hands, I could not believe it; I thought that I had left corruption of the taxi business behind me but here it was again.

On Sunday night I checked the website. It still said Planning Permission Granted, so I convinced myself that the call had been a prank. Early the next morning I looked again, only this time it said Planning Permission Refused, and below was the name 'Mary Goggins'. Comparing the initial Planning Permission Granted print off to the Planning Permission Refused on the screen, it was clearly written by two different people, which meant that either someone had accessed the website stealthily or had entered the Fingal office and posted this refusal.

Anger awakened in me like never before.

'Fucking bastards,' I screamed.

Clare came running into the room.

'What's wrong?' she asked.

'They've replaced the planning grant with a refusal.'

'That's impossible, Tom,' she said. 'They couldn't do that, you already have the grant – you printed it off. There has to be a mistake. Why would they do that?'

I couldn't answer her. Someone had orchestrated this; an individual who wanted to financially destroy me or just someone in Fingal County Council with a grudge. Taking my old tape recorder from the drawer and hooking it up to the phone, I rang Fingal HR department, where the manager confirmed that there was no position for a temporary senior planner, nor had there been postings of any jobs; as my informant had said, Fingal were seeking redundancies. Jotting down the events on a piece of paper, I wrote Mary Goggins's name at the top and a question mark beside who had appointed her. Whoever it was, they would be putting their own career at risk, but perhaps they assumed that the change of permission would go unnoticed and that Aaron Jacobs' replacement would go unchallenged.

I then contacted the Irish Planning Institute, whose recruitment officer would be well versed on the legislation regarding the appointment to government jobs. Speaking with their planning advisor, I relayed my story of planning one day and none the next, and the appointment of Mary Goggins to a position that was neither advertised nor existed. Their pauses and stutters indicated a reluctance to open this Pandora's box, so they simply asked if I wished to make a formal complaint.

Within days, offers from construction companies seeking to tender started to arrive. They must have been watching and had noticed the now phantom grant. The media had no interest in the story, and I eventually found myself sitting in the health clinic in Kilbarrack waiting for Dr Michael Woods, a former Fianna Fáil Minister. Although displaying reservation at what I was telling him, the 2,500-worded grant document convinced him to contact Fingal County Council on my behalf.

Michael returned to me at the start of August saying that Fingal County Council had made a mistake. My heart started to race until he clarified that the mistake had been in posting the grant. Before I could say, 'someone wrote 2,500 words regarding my site and listed every house and contribution by mistake?', he had hung up. All further attempts at correspondence were ignored.

A couple of days later, in a local café, I relayed the story to a reporter who was unfortunate enough to answer his phone.

Overheard by a solicitor seated nearby, Jared Nolan offered his assistance. In his early thirties, he had recently opened a new practice on the northside of Dublin where, within the hour, we were joined by his partner, Barry. Taken aback at my story, they offered to work *pro bono*.

Given that the application was in Clare's name, we were first advised that she should be the one to go through the appeals process, and it was April 2009, almost a year later, by the time all appeals were exhausted and subsequently refused. Coupled with that, An Bord Pleanála (the Irish Planning Appeals Board that determines appeals and other cases under national planning legislation) took no interest in the situation, while at the same time the bank was seeking regular updates. However, all that paled in comparison to the events some weeks later, in May, when on returning home from a night out, Clare and I were greeted with the sounds of sirens and flashing lights coming from the direction of our home. As firemen smashed the upstairs windows with hatchets, flames billowed from the second floor. All Clare and I could do was watch as our house was razed to the ground. With neighbours out in pyjamas offering us blankets, the only consolation was that our sons were away at the time, so no one was injured.

We spent the next few hours with our neighbour, Pat, from whose living room we watched the firemen walk through the burning embers of our home. At 4 a.m., I was interviewed by a Garda Detective who enquired about the cut on my hand. Initially assuming it was out of concern, I soon realised what he was implying and directed him to the CCTV, where he could watch a rerun of the previous evening's activities. Upon further enquiry about money and valuables in the house, I told them that my son Carl had been saving for a deposit for a car and estimated that he had about €10,000 cash in the safe in his wardrobe, and in my own wall safe there were my car keys and about €8,000 cash.

Sunrise came early, and the light that appeared from over our garden wall and caught the yellowish parts of the Howth stone now illuminated the carcass of our home. With her face red and swollen from crying, Clare needed to be removed from the devastation, so we went to one of the unfinished houses in Malahide. By 7 a.m. Clare, and my three dogs, Sabien, Arragjento, Pisa and I were sitting on the concrete floor of 21 Myra Manor as I tried not to dwell on the possibility that the bank might attempt to garnish the insurance monies, given that they were becoming increasingly cash, starved and had already closed off accounts of other developers with whom they were not in dispute. At 9 a.m. my phone rang. Acquaintances in the building trade were generously offering materials and furniture as well as the use of trucks and vans. The most memorable call that day was from Pat, my neighbour, who was looking for a loan of €30,000. Sitting on the concrete floor looking up at roof tiles, I started to laugh.

'My home just burned to the ground and you're looking for a loan?'

'I wouldn't ask but things are hard,' he replied.

My confusion was soon put to one side when Pat informed me that Ian from across the road was interested in buying what was by now a shell of a house. Realising the vultures had already circled, I ended the call.

Sleep deprivation and shock ensured that the remainder of that day was a blur. A taxi driver I had helped in the past and barely remembered showed up with a van and we went to buy beds. By late Sunday night, builders had been arranged to start working the following morning so that the house Clare and I were staying in would be habitable. That same day the Gardaí invited me to the station, and early the next afternoon,

while sitting in an interrogation room, I was presented with
the safes from my home. Enquiring as to whether or not I had
keys, I replied that I had not. Offering to drill them open, the
two Gardaí asked whether I had enemies or financial
problems. Deciding not to allow my mind to wander as far
back as my taxi days, I answered that to the best of my
knowledge I had neither enemies nor financial problems.

'How did you cut your hand, Mr Darcy?' was the next
question, to which I responded that I had already been asked
and answered that question, and what connection had that to
the burning down of my house?

'Just standard questions', I was assured.

'Do you have insurance on your house?' the first Garda
asked.

'Yes.'

'How much is it for?'

'I will show you a copy of the policy,' I offered.

With the safes now open, we found a bundle of half-burnt
cash of which about €5,000 was salvageable. The other safe
as well as the keys to Dillon's and Clare's cars had melted
along with the ashes of thousands more euro.

'How much was in the second safe?' the other Garda asked.

'About €20,000 in total in both safes,' I replied.

'You said €10,000 and €8,000 the other night.'

'I said "about", detective, my bank statements can support
how much.'

Leaving the Garda station, I drove back to Howth. Turning the corner, the magnificent glass structure, which only the
previous week had stood majestically against the backdrop of
Howth Head, was now reduced to burnt ring beams and
blackened glass. I cried walking through the ruins, holding
on tightly to the half-burnt baby pictures and mementos of
my sons' childhoods that I had picked up from the floor.

Immersed in my thoughts, I failed to notice a man approaching me. Bypassing the usual pleasantries, he enquired as to whether I had spoken to Pat, to which I said I had, in the hope that he would go away.

'I know you're probably having difficulties right now with the building industry, so I am willing to offer a good price,' he continued.

I picked up a burnt baby walker and turned to him.

'Get away from me, you parasite.'

'You misunderstand my intentions,' he protested in his pseudo-pretentious Howth accent.

Continuing to glare at him, he eventually turned and walked down the driveway he wanted as his own.

After the June bank holiday weekend, I informed Gordon of the whole sorry event. This was followed by two more meetings, the first in July, where an update on the completion of 21 Myra Manor was sought, and the second, where it was suggested that my solicitor would draft an agreement stating that the insurance monies from Woodview, our family home, would be lodged into the bank's account to be held for us to rebuild our home. In light of Gordon's apparent concern for myself and Clare, and the cordial nature of both meetings, we felt assured of the bank's continued support and that we were still all in this together. However, less than a month later, the bank closed off all my accounts and in doing so put me out of business.

The following month I handed the men their notice. Burdened with the responsibility of families and mortgages, they would break down and cry. Soon, however, self-preservation kicked in, as builders and developers began to turn on each other, demanding by menace monies for works carried out or materials provided. I, too, was to fall victim to the despair of a builder, who having benefited from my generosity, now sought to capitalise on my situation.

Three years earlier, in 2006 my Malahide neighbour, Jimmy Connolly, had stored his containers and machinery on-site, and then in mid-2009 I received a phone call from him.

'Your fence is on my land,' he said, abruptly.

Upon asking him to explain further, his tone grew increasingly aggressive.

'You're stopping me from selling my house!' he shouted.

Apparently the temporary fence I had erected was six inches into his land. I assured him that it would be moved back a metre. Driving home to Myra Manor that evening, I passed the house whose sale I was allegedly preventing. More likely, it appeared that my neighbour had run out of money, for it stood half built with neither windows nor doors and a driveway with open potholes and abandoned machinery. Amused at the thought of my little fence preventing a sale, I nonetheless organised for the fencing company to set back the fence one metre, which gave him twenty-two square metres of free land. In spite of which, less than three weeks later, I received a registered letter which would remove the humour of my neighbour's accusation. A small man, dressed in an oversized coat, knocked on my door and asked for me by name. Upon confirming who I was, he handed me the post.

'You're served,' he said, and walked away.

Assuming it was from my bank, I then noticed the name at the top, Jimmy Connolly. My former building colleague was suing me for €450,000, claiming that I was preventing the sale of his property. My life was collapsing around me: my home had burnt to the ground, I was living in a half-finished building with no income and now I was facing bankruptcy if I did not concede to these demands. But for the next week I had to leave this matter aside and return to the issue with Fingal County Council who had pulled planning permission on Waterside.

On 28 August 2009, at 2.30 p.m., I walked into Fingal County Council and delivered the summons identifying the judicial review on behalf on my wife. I was only back in my hall door when the phone rang and a blocked number appeared. Congratulating me, I was informed by a jolly voice on the other end that I had caused a 'shit storm'. The same man, who had initially informed me that planning had been pulled went on to tell me that 'they're running for cover'. He was laughing so loudly, he was hardly able to contain himself.

'Mary Goggins has been hauled in and so has Aaron Jacobs. Good on you, hope you expose these fuckers,' and he rang off.

Two hours later, at 4.40 p.m., Gordon rang. Having relieved himself of the new face of banking persona, Clare and I were instructed to be in head office at 10 a.m. the following Tuesday. With no explanation given, we were told to 'just be there, both of you'.

Although I had not been completely open with Clare about the developments and the security they held, I knew she had not signed any documents relating to our home, so at least we would have a roof over our heads. Unwilling to spend that weekend dissecting and analysing every potential scenario and outcome, I decided not to tell Clare about the meeting until Monday morning, fearing that we would just start to argue. Indeed, when faced with difficulties, our differences had now grown so vast that we were practically strangers to the teenagers who had fallen in love. Now, just moments of the nostalgic love that once bound us together continued to flicker within the embers of our memories.

The self-inflicted guilt I carried as a result of my decision to go into property development was physically obvious when I looked in the mirror early that Monday morning. The reflection was older but showed the familiar feelings of a decade earlier: self-hatred and loathing for another course of action that could ruin my family. I stood at the door of our bedroom and gazed at Clare asleep. Her stillness and the angelic face that had once captured my heart was oblivious to what awaited her, as she would soon awaken to a nightmare of fear and uncertainty. Another cavern in the massive void within my heart opened. It was sadness beyond understanding as my eyes watered and tears fell like the heavens had opened. Silently I whispered, 'I'm sorry' and returned to the bathroom to calm my emotions.

After breakfast I took a call from a contractor but pretended it was from Gordon. 'He wants us over in Ballsbridge tomorrow,' I said to Clare.

'Why?' she replied.

'Don't know,' I answered, as I was already preoccupied with the looming American stock market crisis and its potential effect on the Irish property market. We talked until late into night about possible reasons for the meeting, and by the next morning we felt assured that we had covered every eventuality. Walking into the head office of AIB in Ballsbridge at 10 a.m., we were instructed by the receptionist to wait for Gordon, who soon appeared in his banker's suit. The tone had changed. There were neither smiles nor small talk.

'They're waiting for you in the conference room,' he said, ushering us through a large door where two unfamiliar men were seated.

'We all know why we're here,' Gordon began. Clare looked at me with confusion.

'I don't,' I interjected.

'I'm Kevin Daly, the credit manager,' said one of the men, 'and I'm going to tell you what's going to happen now.'

At which point he held three fingers up in the air.

'One, you're going to drop the judicial review against

Fingal County Council. Two, you're going to drop the investigation by the Irish Planning Institute. Three, we're appointing Paul Cody to take over your development and bring it to completion. You won't be using your staff, Paul will appoint his own.'

'Who is Paul Cody?' I asked.

'He is the former head of Dún Laoghaire-Rathdown County Council,' Daly snapped back.

Paul Cody had also been a figure in the Mahon Tribunal, during which he had been questioned by Mr Justice Flood regarding his relationship with the disgraced lobbyist Frank Dunlop. Apparently suffering from amnesia, coupled with the unavailability of resources for note taking, it appeared that no written evidence existed of any alleged meetings. Furthermore, Paul Cody had been a friend and a former work colleague of Dennis Jackson, administration officer with Fingal County Council planning section and boss to Mary Goggins.

It had been less than three hours from the issuing of the judicial review summons to Fingal County Council when I had been notified of this meeting. Now I was being told that the former head of another county council, who was also a former work colleague of the chief planner in Fingal County Council, was taking over my development at Waterside.

'What if we don't agree?' Clare asked.

Daly leaned over the table as far as his large stomach would allow.

'We have very deep pockets,' he said, 'and we will make you homeless.'

Shocked, my wife sank back into her seat. Sensing our vulnerability, I realised that the only option was to behave passively, so I said that we would do as requested if my workers could be re-employed.

'Absolutely not,' Daly retorted.

Given that many of my staff were good friends, I asked for a letter of explanation so they would be assured that I had not chosen to let them go without good reason. Daly agreed and everyone left, leaving Clare and I alone.

Gordon reappeared at the door.

'At least we're still working together,' he assured us.

Although it appeared that my initial fears about the bank pulling the plug had been unfounded, I still had mixed feelings. Anxieties were high as we walked back to the car and the trip home was silent. Passing the toll bridge, I remembered the young couple with their three sons on New Year's Eve 2000 looking forward to their new beginning. Sadness filled my heart for being so blind to the riches I never realised I had. Clare interrupted my thoughts.

'Can he put us on the street? Is our family home at risk?' she asked.

'You heard him,' I replied. 'They're developing my portfolio.'

I tried to tone down the situation but nonetheless felt ashamed at the way I had allowed Daly to threaten my wife while humiliating me, and I still needed to ring Paul Cody (who had been appointed to take over my development) in the hope that some of my men would be re-employed. Later that day, Cody told me that having spoken to the bank as well as Fingal County Council, it had been arranged that I was to address the planning board of Fingal County Council to assure them that the judicial review would be dropped. It appeared that a meeting had been arranged prior to the events that morning at AIB. When enquiring about my contractors and architect, I was told by Cody that he had his own team. An hour later, I phoned Jared Nolan & Company Solicitors to inform them that the judicial review was being dropped.

So this was what the Mahon Tribunal had been all about: collusion between local authorities and banks. In my case, it was AIB appointing the former head of Dún Laoghaire-Rathdown County Council to take over the Waterside development, while forcing Clare and me to withdraw a judicial review against his friends and former colleagues. In the post the next day, I was officially informed of the appointment of Paul Cody, former head of Dún Laoghaire-Rathdown County Council as the new developer of Waterside. Opening the envelope I smiled, thinking how arrogant Daly had been to put such information into a letter that would eventually become prime evidence in my claim against AIB for deceit and fraud.

The next day I met Jared in the Law Library, where, in a quiet corner shielded by an oak divider, I updated him on events.

'They cannot do that, Tom. They can't force you to drop a judicial review with threats,' he protested, at which point I rang Gordon.

'I want to clarify yesterday's meeting,' I said calmly. 'I must drop the judicial review and investigation by the Irish Planners Institute and accept Paul Cody's appointment to take over my development or else I will be made homeless?'

Gordon paused.

'Yes, Tom, that's my understanding of what you were informed of yesterday.'

Visibly shaken, Jared was seething after listening to Gordon.

'I'm bloody furious, Tom,' he said, 'we have put a lot of time and money into this. Surely you're not considering dropping the case?'

He looked at me awaiting an emphatic, 'no'.

'I have no choice,' I murmured. 'They can take my home.'

'That's ludicrous, Tom,' he tried to reassure me.

I could see that he was desperately trying to hold onto this case, which could launch his firm into the public arena, but I had my family to think of. Standing up to leave, Jared informed me of impending legal fees that could reach €12,000.

'I thought you were working *pro bono?*' I said.

'That was until you pulled the case, Tom. We have to get paid for all the work we have done now that we are not going to get our day in court.'

Assuring him that payment would be made, I shook his hand for the last time. The following week, Paul Cody reiterated that he would be using his own team, but eventually conceded that my architect would be kept on – though this was less due to my own insistence and more the result of my architect refusing to sign off on the plans and threatening to report any architect who did so to the Royal Institute of the Architects of Ireland (RIAI).

That Thursday morning, 10 September, I parked outside the offices of Fingal County Council to meet Paul Cody. Pulling up beside me, a tall man alighted from a green Jaguar – in his mid-sixties and dressed in a banker's navy suit. Upon introduction, I was met with specific orders. Tilting his head downward, he spoke as if to instruct a child entering a neighbour's home.

'When we go in here, you are going to stand up and tell them that the judicial review is gone, the investigation is over,' he said.

So here it was, a piece of drama in which I had been assigned the role of obedient servant whose purpose was to conceal the corruption being perpetrated against me.

Walking into Fingal County Council offices, I felt my dignity compromised and shame for what I was about to do. The Chinese tattoo of integrity etched across my shoulder symbolised all a man should be. Now with a heavy heart, I convinced myself that there was no other option. Paul and I walked up the spiral staircase and turned left at the top, where my orders were repeated. Sitting around the table were three men in their late thirties and a fourth in his fifties, whom Paul introduced by their Christian names. Straight to business, Paul addressed the board.

'Tom has a few words to say, and then we can get down to business.'

I cleared the taste of disgust from my throat and repeated my orders with as much feigned sincerity as could be mustered, while their smirks and smiles grew wider with each reassuring word. I stood, after surrendering my self-respect and honour, subdued into defeat and mentally accusing them of corruption and deceit. Which one of them had appointed Mary Goggins? I wondered. How thick that carpet must be with the increasing amount of deception being swept under it.

Paul stood and reassured the group.

'Now that that's sorted, let's put it behind us. Tom's dropping all that nonsense, so we can get back on track.'

'What type of houses are you going to apply for in the new planning application?' interrupted the overweight man in a well-worn grey suit.

Ignorant of the scalded looks directed at him, one of the younger men present informed us that Paul was putting together a new set of plans which would be available the following week. Ten minutes later, with assurances accepted that it was just a formality of the new plans being lodged and granted – the same planning that had been stolen from me – we exchanged more loose handshakes and we were back on the street.

'I will get those plans done by next week and come back to you,' Paul told me.

That was the last time we met. Over the coming weeks, my calls and emails to both Paul and the bank were ignored until I finally caught him with my number blocked.

'Look, I have no instructions from the bank, don't call me again,' he said and rang off.

With Christmas just weeks away, my former staff called begging for work. Stories of their children's Santa lists, mortgages in arrears and impending poverty affected me deeply. Such was the financial strain on their relationships that for many of them Christmas 2009 would be the last with their family.

For the first time in my own life, I was unable to earn a living. The building industry had collapsed, and to compensate for reduced earnings, some builders were under-pricing work and then extracting money from unsuspecting people who trusted that the original quote was the total amount, only to be told that another €5,000–€10,000 was needed halfway through the build. With the prospect of an abandoned half-finished wall or bathroom, they would often be held to ransom.

With no work, I resorted to selling our family goods. Car payments mounted up until they were repossessed, and garden ornaments were sold to fund the next affidavit, motion or appeal. I tried the outdoor markets in North County Dublin, filling the van at 6 a.m. every Sunday morning in the hope that enough money would be made to get us through the week. My first visit was just after the monies raised from the copper salvaged from the debris of my home ran out. It was an exotic world of open markets where people from all nations gathered to pick up a bargain. Most of the items were second-hand: shoes, dresses, prams and coats. The stall cost €30 with another €10 needed for diesel to bring the last remnants of our home to be displayed on a table made from marine plywood. It was mainly Nigerians and Bosnians who offered €10 for a €200 cordless DeWalt drill, standing at times for half an hour, arguing with me if they didn't get what they wanted. Most days the rain sent me home before I had made any money.

By March 2010, I had received a court date from Jimmy Connolly's solicitor to attend court in July. He was seeking €450,000 in compensation plus costs for trespass. Then soon after, on 27 April, I received a demand letter from AIB for €17.5 million. They were calling in my loans, €10 million for the site in Howth that was to become Waterside, €4.5 million for the two Myra Manor properties and €3 million in interest. This was my first contact with AIB since I had met Paul Cody who had been appointed to take over my development. It is worth mentioning that to this day the site that was to be Waterside has remained undeveloped and the properties in Myra Manor are unfinished, which was contrary to the agreement made eight months earlier.

Three weeks later, while walking home from the shops with groceries for that day, a silver Ford Focus pulled up beside Clare and me. A man in his early twenties asked if I was Tom Darcy, and then served a special summons from the bank seeking possession of my home. (The word possession is used in this book to refer to the order of a court for possession of a family home).

That evening was filled with fear. Unable to watch Clare crying, I ended up leaving Myra Manor in the early hours, allowing me some emotional distance. By 4 a.m., I found myself in Howth, seven miles from Myra Manor but only yards from my true home in Woodview. I thought of my sons fast asleep and unaware of the attack being mounted against the family. As I watched a trawler leaving the harbour, with the sun now rising and illuminating the vessel breaking waves beneath its bow, I wondered how it would feel to escape into the stillness of the sea that returned as the trawler disappeared. I remembered my childhood in Silver Strand, Wicklow, in the 1970s, and how in the early hours I would go fishing on an extended rock of ninety metres in length from the shore into the sea, known locally as the Long Rock. Sitting at its end, the waves would make soft, soothing noises, isolating me from a world from which I sought to escape. How I wished I could return and change everything.

The following week I received a letter from the solicitor for AIB regarding the proposed insurance settlement from the fire at our home. They wanted to make a court order of the contract that had been agreed by our solicitors a few months earlier. This required the lodgement of the insurance monies into an account in the bank – and then on production of an architect's certificate, the monies would be released to rebuild Woodview. However, I knew it was a Trojan horse because they already had a contract, so why would they want it made into a High Court order? Our solicitor, at that time, Ivor Fitzpatrick, advised us to agree, and three weeks later Mr Justice Roderick Murphy made it an order.

During the following weeks I received more demand notices and solicitors' letters. A contractor, who I had employed for years, was now suing me, claiming that I had not paid him enough. I felt his desperation, although it saddened me to think that our friendship meant so little to him. Assuming a direct approach could clear up the issue, I phoned him telling him I had no money and the bank was suing me too. His reply was not the first time I would witness how people discard their moral compass as they suffer from selective amnesia.

'You have your insurance money from your home,' he shouted back. 'Give me that.'

It appeared that the vultures were waiting to feast on what remnants would be left after the bank had finished with me.

'Sue me all you like,' I said. 'My books show your men leaving the site every Thursday at 11 a.m. and not returning until 2 p.m. Would they have been collecting social welfare? You see, Seán, I was only responsible for my workers' taxes, not the subcontractors. That was your responsibility. I have their names and addresses.'

The line went silent.

'It was a pity you weren't in the fuckin' house when it burnt, you bastard. Rot in hell.'

By July I was in front of Mr Justice Brian McGovern in the High Court for Jimmy Connolly's trespass case. A friend had told me that I would lose because the fence was on his land originally. Advising me to make him an offer, we sold most of Clare's jewellery and my own watch and ring, and eventually raised €9,000 from a 'friend', who, aware of the situation, paid less than 70 per cent of the market value for the jewellery. Although caring little for my own possessions, Clare's had sentimentality attached to each piece. Upon hearing of my offer, Connolly smiled.

'In your dreams,' he said. 'I'm going to get half a mil today.'

Inside Court 6, the disdain shown by the judge towards lay litigants was obvious (an individual who has no legal representation and is forced to represent themselves in court). The case being heard before mine was that of a builder in debt. Pleading with broken speech and watched on by his wife and two children, he begged the judge not to make him bankrupt, but, without hesitation, a flick of the gavel initiated the man's nightmare. My case was next. Connolly's barrister stood up and rhymed off all the money his client had lost due to the 'trespass' committed by me. The mere inches taken by the temporary fence sounded like acres, while the description of the derelict building without windows and rusting machinery that now served as garden ornaments could have been mistaken for a

bespoke house with cultivated parkland. When he had finished
the judge asked me how I pleaded. I stood up and said, 'not
guilty', which were my first words uttered in an Irish court.

Judge McGovern's annoyance at my feeble attempt to raise
a defence was obvious.

'But what's your defence, Mr Darcy?' he repeated.

I claimed that the fence was only a temporary fixture and
that the plaintiff's claim was merely a vexatious attempt to
extract monies from me. Throughout the proceedings
Connolly sat at the back of the courtroom smiling. Judge
McGovern finally made his ruling in Connolly's favour, based
on the fact that the fence was at one time encroaching on his
land, albeit by six inches. However, the cheers from the back
of the court soon fell to silence when it was ruled that
compensation to the plaintiff should be €4,000 plus costs.

I ignored Connolly outside the courtroom, remembering
the generosity I had extended to him and how his behaviour
had made Clare and me sell items from when we were young
lovers. The following day I bought back some of Clare's
jewellery with added interest applied.

'It's not personal, just business, sure you would do the same
yourself, Tom,' said the man whom I had once considered a
good friend.

I glared into his eyes.

'I would have given you the money and never asked for it
back,' I replied with a mixture of anger and sadness.

Three weeks later, Connolly's solicitors sent me an invoice
seeking €45,000 in costs, which included the €4,000 in
compensation and €41,000 in legal costs. At the end was
written: payment to be made within five days or bankruptcy
will be sought. Two weeks later I was back in front of Judge
McGovern pleading not to be made bankrupt, knowing that
my bank would get all my assets, including our family home,

and I couldn't defend it. For once you are made bankrupt you surrender your free will to an assignee to manage your affairs. With my heart beating out of my chest, the court listened to Connolly's barrister playing up the figure.

'Mr Darcy, do you have the money here today to pay Mr Connolly?' Judge McGovern asked me.

'Yes, Judge I have the €4,000'.

'Mr Darcy, do you have the €41,000 legal fees as well?'

I shook my head.

'Then I declare you bankrupt.'

Retreating to the gents, I knelt down over a toilet and vomited. That afternoon I called our solicitors to inform them. They were furious, though not at the prospect of losing our home but us because they may not get paid. The next morning the assignee from the court arrived. Tall, and with the air of an undertaker, he walked straight in with clipboard in hand.

'I'm Tony, your assignee,' he said. 'This is going to be difficult, but you can get through it.'

Moving throughout our home he noted furniture and other items. Never did I feel as helpless and ashamed as when I watched this stranger calculate my life's worth. It was only when he asked to see Clare's jewellery that I saw red. Smashing my fist through the glass door, I looked at him like I wanted to cut his throat with the shards of glass at my feet. Hurrying to the door, he said he would return on Friday.

The following Friday, 22 October, I received a letter from Fingal County Council seeking planning fees for 17 Myra Manor that had remained derelict for over a year and a half. Together with the demands for money from desperate former friends, I was looking at over €160,000 in civil bills and demand letters. Still reeling from the shock, I heard a voice behind me.

'Morning, Mr Darcy.'

Tony, the assignee, had let himself into my home.

'I have come to take an inventory of your upstairs and attic.'

No tea was offered nor hospitality that would ordinarily be extended to a guest. This man wanted to sell all the sentimental belongings from our lives – pennies for items that had cost thousands.

'How does your salary get paid?' I asked him.

'I'm a civil servant and get paid like any other civil servant,' he replied. 'The sale of your things doesn't impact on whether I get paid or not. The court gets the first payment from the sale of assets and items sold, then your creditors'.

'You will be with me for the next twelve years, is that correct?' I continued.

'Yes,' he replied. 'I will adjudicate over your finances until your release from bankruptcy.'

So I would never be free of this man. Every move or business decision that I wanted to make would have to be discussed with him first, like a child seeking permission from a parent.

'Twelve years,' I said aloud, my mind questioning all possibilities. 'What if my mother leaves me something in her will in ten years' time or I get a pay increase if I have a job?'

'You're in this for twelve years,' Tony replied, like a prison warden to a new inmate. However, unlike an inmate, there would be no possibility of temporary release, three meals per day or free TV and utilities.

'How much do you spend on food?' I was then asked. Upon hearing that my three Saint Bernard dogs cost about €30 per week, he estimated that at €1,500 per year plus veterinary costs they would have to go, at which point I lost it.

'Listen to me, Tony, those dogs are like my kids to me, so don't tell me I have to get rid of them. Would you get rid of your children?'

I could taste the hatred I had for him.

'Get out, just get the fuck out of my home.' I opened the door and he scurried out like a rabbit.

'This is not going away, Mr Darcy,' he shouted back.

I slammed the door shut causing the house to shake. Clare ran in from the kitchen.

'I told that parasite to get out.'

Her disapproving glare angered me further, but when I told her that he wanted us to get rid of Sabien, Arragjento and Pisa, the same tone turned into tears and she slowly sank to the floor.

But good news was on the way. The following week our solicitor, Ivor Fitzpatrick, informed us that the insurance company wanted to talk. Aware that the building costs would be taken by the bank, the contents cover was our own. So in the first week in November, in the Law Library in the Four Courts in Dublin, we sat round a table to thrash out a deal: the bank's representative, our barristers, solicitors, Clare and I. Every few minutes the barrister would return with a counter offer from the insurance company, 50 per cent less than what had been claimed the first time, until it was agreed that the building costs would be matched for what was claimed, and so we ended up with €50,000. What I did not realise at the time was that our solicitor was also representing AIB and the insurance company. Months earlier one of the senior partners in Ivor Fitzpatrick & Company Solicitors had advised us not to bother defending the bank's claim: 'Sure you can't get blood from a stone, give them everything and start again.' In hindsight I wonder which client Ivor Fitzpatrick was truly representing.

Clare and I looked at each other. We knew it would cost €45,000 to buy our way out of bankruptcy, which would leave €5,000. Taking a moment outside the room, I explained to her what being in bankruptcy would mean for the next twelve years, so we agreed to hand over the money. Two weeks later the solicitor for Connolly received his cheque for €45,000, €4,000 of which went to Connolly. We were out of bankruptcy, and that same week the bank got the cheque from the insurance company for €650,000 for the rebuild of Woodview, our family home.

During the last week in November my brother Dermot unexpectedly arrived at my home. Having not seen each other for over fifteen years, the pain of rejection and hurt awakened like a volcano, for my family's story was characterised by drink and abuse, rivalry and favouritism. Age had taken its toll on my brother's frame, but he still had the smile that always warmed my heart. I expected that he had come to tell me that my mum or dad had passed away; however, it was my brother, Freddie, who had died from a brain haemorrhage. Even though such a long time had passed, I always thought Freddie, Dermot and I would reconcile our issues. Dermot and I hugged awkwardly for the first time in our lives; like strangers we did not know how to show our feelings. He told me of the funeral arrangements and left, while my sons held me as I wept. The palpable grief for an estranged brother released every emotion bottled up within me after years of protecting myself from the pain of not feeling good enough within my family. I went to Freddie's funeral and then left, not wanting to cause trouble or resurrect old wounds, a decision I regret every waking moment.

The personal toll of unemployment in the lives of former employees was beginning to show. Men with mortgages and families to support were left destitute. Some, unable to carry the burden of shame, took their own lives. One of whom was a young man of thirty-two who had worked on my site for seven years. Curly and I occasionally shared stories at lunchtime as he hung over the scaffolding enjoying a cigarette. I had congratulated him on his engagement to his girlfriend, the purchase of their home together, marriage and then becoming a father, and I finally held him as he cried in my arms the day I had to end his employment.

It was this image that replayed in my mind while following his coffin into the church, where I met the men who had greeted Curly on-site every morning. Philip Jenkins, another contractor, walked over.

'You've some balls showing up here, Tom Darcy,' he said. 'You should be ashamed of yourself.'

'I came to pay my respects to a friend. I don't want any hassle,' I replied. Lunging forward to strike me, he was caught by Mark, an electrician who had also worked with Curly.

'Phil, leave it out, Tom's not the enemy.'

The media had portrayed developers as the cause of the misery that befell this country, but this was the first time I was attacked by one of my own.

Sitting at the back of the church, I heard the priest call Curly by his Christian name, Brendan 'A father and loving husband, an incredible son and friend; all who met him loved him, but his short, young life was lost to his torments.'

Curly had not worked since becoming unemployed, and his home was in the process of being possessed. As a result he had spiralled into a depression. Then, one morning, while sitting on the pier at 4 a.m., he had downed a bottle of Jack Daniels and swallowed two bottles of sleeping tablets. A jogger found his body later the same day. I thought of how lonely Curly must have felt sitting on the pier away from his wife and the children he loved. How terrible his mindset must have been to take that final action. Glancing at the Stations of the Cross and the crucifixion of Christ, I thought of the cross of mental torture that was being imposed upon those who had committed no crimes. These were the people who carried the invisible crown of thorns until they were unable to bear the pain any longer. I left as the priest blessed Brendan's coffin, closing the door on the cries of the mourners.

Waking the following morning from another restless sleep, resentment and anger simmered as I lay and watched the dark sky lighten. By 9 a.m., I was reading over the special summons the bank had sent me when the phone rang. I assumed it was someone looking for money or a warning of the termination of one of the utilities, but instead it was Daly from the bank.

'Which house was your family home?'

I answered that it was Woodview in Howth. 'Doesn't matter, this is your last Christmas in it.' He laughed and rang off.

It was five days before Christmas 2010, and we had little more than €4,000 left from the insurance claim. With no income and few items left from our home to sell, my son Greg had made an application for social welfare. However, upon arrival at our home, the assessment officer came to a conclusion.

'You would need to have money to run this house.'

Granted, from the outside looking in, the property we inhabited gave the appearance of a certain lifestyle, but in reality we were asset rich and cash poor.

Perhaps at these times in a person's life they turn to their family. Tragically, it had been over twenty years since issues with my parents had become so unfixable that I stopped visiting them. Ostracised by my brothers and sister, and with my sons' christenings, communions and confirmations missed and eighteenth birthdays and graduations lost, as well as my own birthdays, the true story of my childhood was the burden I carried, ring-fenced from even those closest to me; a vulnerability so great it could diminish me in seconds if tipped upon. Each Christmas, Mother's Day and on my mum's birthday, I would go straight to her voicemail. I feared rejection if I spoke to her directly or that she would just hang up and compound the rejection already felt. What had become an automatic script repeated on each occasion, I repeated that Christmas Eve.

I found a place somewhere away from everyone and called her.

'Hi Mum, it's your prodigal son. Hope you're okay and you have a good Christmas. Love you, miss you, Tommy.'

The message also mentioned how much I missed and regretted not seeing Freddie. Sitting on the floor of the attic holding the mobile phone, I listened to Christmas songs coming from downstairs. Mum's favourite song, 'Ave Maria', reverberated through the floorboards. I closed my eyes and saw her crying as she always did when listening to that song. Now it held as much sentimental meaning for me as it had for her. When it ended I wiped away my tears just like I had seen her do many times before, her hand touching her eyes, with a forced smile as she looked at me saying how silly she was. The pain of those memories showed me how much I missed her. I composed myself and washed my face. Looking into the mirror, I wished life could have been different.

Walking back down the stairs, the beep of a phone message interrupted my thoughts. Looking at the screen of the mobile, my heart raced, realising it was my mum's house number. I pressed 171 to access my voicemail, holding the phone close to my ear, not wanting to miss a word of the softness of her voice, but instead my father's voice startled me. As though ordering a pint of Guinness, a sentence repeated thousands of times in his life, he said without emotion: 'Your mother is in heaven.'

My legs gave way from under me. I dropped the phone, grabbed the handrail and staggered to my room. Falling onto my bed, I cried uncontrollably. 'How? When?' I kept thinking, only to be interrupted by Carl.

'Are you okay?' He shouted to Dillon and Clare to come quick, but I just wanted to be left alone. For my sons this was the second time in as many weeks for them to witness their father in such an emotional state.

I stammered, 'My mum's dead.' To them, she was a grandmother they barely knew, a part of their dad's life that had caused him such pain. To Clare, my mother was alien to everything she held dear. She couldn't understand how a mother could ignore her own son, not care about him and ostracise him and her grandchildren. In Clare's eyes she was not normal.

'When did she die?' Clare asked.

I just pressed my voicemail on speaker so she could hear my father's message. Dillon left the room and returned with his laptop.

'There is no listing for your mum in RIP.ie,' he said, assuming that her passing had been recent. Strange, I thought, how her song had played earlier, and I wondered if she was contacting me spiritually.

Dillon interrupted my thoughts. 'Your mum died in May 2009.'

I stared at him in disbelief, shaking my head. Dermot had not said a word but then I never asked him how my mother was. Oh my God, I never asked him. The reality that I never asked him kept repeating in my mind. He just spoke of Freddie in the short time he was in my home. I took the laptop from Dillon and looked at the obituary. She had died the month my home burnt to the ground and nobody had told me. I had left birthday and Christmas wishes as well as Mother's Day greetings for over eighteen months and nobody told me.

'Why did Dermot not tell me?' I asked aloud.

'He must have thought you knew and didn't go to the funeral,' Clare replied.

'What kind of people don't tell their brother or son that their mother has died? Men who commit the most heinous of crimes are allowed out of prison to bury their mothers.'

Eventually my tears slowed and anger filled my heart. From the grave she had shown me the ultimate rejection that had been supported by my father, brother and sister. Their inaction spoke volumes of their lack of humanity towards me and to this day has left me with the inability to love, trust or believe in anyone. From that evening until January was a haze for me. During the following weeks more solicitors' letters and summonses arrived along with dates for court, but I was detached from life as I questioned the kind of human being I was.

A week after Christmas my brother Dermot's wife, Angela, arrived at our home. Not having seen her for over fifteen years, I hardly recognised her. The young woman standing beside her was my niece, whom I hadn't seen since she was five years old. Starting to cry, Angela told me that Dermot had passed away suddenly from an embolism. Shock took over me.

'When?' I whispered.

'Two weeks ago.'

I stared at her in disbelief.

'He's dead and buried and you're telling me now?'

'Dermot didn't want you to find out the way you did about your mother,' she replied.

Angela's parting promise was the only comfort I had received in all the deaths in my family, and that was for me to partake in the scattering of Dermot's ashes on the Long Rock in Wicklow, where he too dreamed of his nirvana. Taking my number, she promised to ring but never did.

From that evening until early February I lived as a zombie. By mid-February the bank had got a summary judgement in my absence, even though Clare had phoned them and explained my losses. Hoping for an adjournment, their refusal exposed the heartless vultures that hid behind their Louis Copeland suits. However, it was the civil summons in March that brought me to my senses and the possession proceedings for our home that had been granted in my absence.

Rummaging through a mountain of letters and civil summonses, I came across a solicitor's letter. My former credit union was suing me for €70,000, claiming that the €100 that I had donated a year earlier to save jobs was a payment on a loan account that had lain dormant for ten years. The court date of the summons was the following morning. Another letter from Fingal County Council claimed that loose debris was flying from our family home in Woodview and posed a danger to the surrounding area. They, too, were threatening to bring me to court if the matter was not addressed. How ironic that due to their corrupt actions I had lost planning permission, then they played along with the Paul Cody 'Dog and pony show' in order to ensure that I dropped the judicial review and investigation, and now they were threatening me. Then there was another letter from the bank requesting a building contract and saying that they wanted to open an account for the insurance monies. Since it had been three months already, that was €5,000 in lost interest. I immediately phoned Dillon, who had been my project manager for five years, and told him about the request. Having recently established a new building company, a boost would help him with this fresh start.

That night in the hope of sleep I closed my eyes but was nonetheless disturbed by potential courtroom scenarios the following day. Unprepared, I hoped for an adjournment; that hearing of the sudden passing of my immediate family members, the judge would defer on compassionate grounds.

By 7 a.m. I was walking around the back garden with Sabien, the alpha male of his pack. With my arms around him, I wondered if I too would be able to look after my family.

Walking into Court 23 at 10.30 a.m., the black heavy doors opened to reveal a room full of men, women and children displaying a collective look of anxiety, as barristers fluttered around and solicitors flipped through papers. Angus Cleary from the credit union could be seen engaging with his counsel. Then the judge emerged from his chambers and settled himself.

I noted the cases in my notebook, whilst at the same time the barrister for AB Wolfe Debt Collection Services, on behalf of Bank of Ireland, was listing his cases. In that hour alone he gained judgements against thirty people, all for billable hours. These are the hours it takes to write letters to the homeowner from the bank and their legal team, the first of which would be sent on behalf of the bank, informing their customer of arrears and usually costing €200 per letter (a standard of three letters sent). The second letter is from the bank's solicitor and the third is written by the debt collection agency's own solicitor issuing proceedings against the borrower. Such is the ingenuity of this plan that should the borrower be unable to pay (and made bankrupt as a result), the bank can claim the loss as a tax relief against future gains. Indeed, the banks, solicitors and debt collection agencies can claim a minimum of €7,500 in legal costs against small borrowers. Multiply that by thirty cases per hour, six hours per day, five days per week, forty-two weeks per year and with an average of twenty district courts around Ireland, the total number is staggering.

Then there is the cost of delivering the summons itself, which apparently requires the participation of the server whose job includes knocking on the door of the borrower, whose unemployed status is the direct result of the criminal behaviour of the same banks pursuing him/her and whose fear now makes them play hide-and-seek behind the curtains. After three attempts the server can go next door and ask the neighbour if they know of the occupant's whereabouts, no doubt relaying the reason for their enquiry. This is followed by the cost of the barrister and the solicitor who attend court in order to claim for the sending of the letter. Eventually, permission is sought from the judge to send the letter by ordinary post of 70 cent, though not before the legal team receives €1,250 for the initial attempts.

As the first hour passes, twenty similar cases are presented to the court. It appears that the queens and kings from another country have allowed those in black gowns and wigs to claim €25,000 for an hour's work, totalling tens of millions, all paid by the persecuted Irish taxpayers. Such is the travesty of the Irish legal system where common sense appears too common to be administered.

Abandoning my notepad when my name was called, I listened to the barrister for the credit union summarise her claim against me with reference to the loan I had taken out. After denying me an adjournment regardless of my lack of counsel, which I claimed violated my right to a fair trial, I explained to the court how this loan had been taken out over ten years previously and as such was statute barred, meaning that six years had lapsed since the last payment was received and so legal proceedings could not be issued. Angus Cleary, however, implied that I had voluntarily started to service the loan, thereby breaking the statute.

What had happened was that back in 1999 I had borrowed IR£40,000 from the credit union, and together with my shares of IR£23,000 and other savings, I had bought a taxi licence for IR£73,000. A year later the taxi industry was deregulated which rendered taxi licences worthless. Since the credit union wanted the licence in their name, I had given them power of attorney.

Then in 2000, the credit union tried to sue me but, given that they were barred from issuing commercial loans, realised that they had broken the law.

Fast forward to 2010 when the new manager was going through their books and contacted me under the guise of looking for donations to save the jobs of two women who, having worked there for the past twenty years, were about to be let go. I offered the €100 I got for an industrial steam cleaner, which was the 'repayment' he was referring to, and it would not surprise me if he had applied this tactic with other customers as well.

Angus Cleary took the stand and told the court that I had contacted the credit union and started to service the loan, omitting the fact that my account had been closed. I had also been unemployed for two years, so would have been unable to make payments even if I had wanted to. Upon cross–examination I asked who had made the initial contact, to which he admitted that it had been himself. Upon further enquiry about how he came into possession of my mobile number after ten years, he said that it had been in the files, at which point I asked why in the last ten years the credit union had not contacted me. Angus Cleary could not answer, nor could he explain how I made the payment before Christmas. I offered possible scenarios, like I had filled in a lodgement slip, or perhaps I had left €100 in the accountant's office and wrote my name on the envelope for the fund to save the jobs he had lied about. However, regardless of his inability to answer my questions, a judgment was granted against me. As a result of which, I started an investigation that would expose the hundreds of millions of euro of taxpayer's money lining the pockets of the same banks that continue to lie to the Irish people.

By June 2011 we had obtained planning permission to demolish and rebuild Woodview along with a High Court order

that required AIB to pay the insurance monies on production
of an architect's certificate as soon as the building was
complete. Dillon took over the build and received construction
materials from the supplier who trusted him that they would
be paid. Gordon was furnished with a commencement notice
at the start of July and works began. Within six weeks our home
was demolished and rebuilt to the first floor level. However,
two weeks after the first architect's certificate was issued, AIB
refused to honour it. Work stopped and unable to pay the men
and suppliers, Dillon's reputation was ruined. For the next eight
months dozens of emails and letters were sent demanding that
AIB honour their agreement and obey the High Court order
but they never did. Dillion has not worked since.

As the court date for the possession of our home loomed
closer, and with no money to pay a solicitor, I tried to access
information from various sources. A representative of the Free
Legal Advice Centres (FLAC) not only told me that they
could not speak to me for six months, but, given the
circumstances of my case, it was unlikely that they could afford
to take me on. My local Citizens Information Centre was the
next port of call, where I stood in line behind others seeking
similar advice. Such were the crowds that had gathered from
early morning there was rarely a seat vacant. Glancing around,
the look of despair etched upon the faces of men and women
bore testimony to the prospect of homelessness now becoming
rampant throughout Ireland. Regardless of the well-meaning
staff dispensing advice, they did not have the knowledge of
the law necessary to support someone defending their home.
All that was left to do was to try and piece together a defence
myself to legally stop the sheriff and his men doing to my
home what I had seen him do to others.

Back home, in front of my computer, I spent months
trawling the internet in search of the weaponry that could

shield those I loved from such pain. By the early hours, exhaustion would take hold, but then adrenaline kicked in as memories of other evictions came to mind and I would be jolted back to attention. With less than ten days to the court hearing, I opened an email that claimed to be from an Irish barrister. As requested, I sent him the documents relating to the case in hard copy, which he promised to read over the weekend if he received them the same day. The cost of photocopying alone was €24, which was three days food for my family. By 2 p.m., I had handed the folder in to the reception desk in the Law Library with the name Daniel O'Keefe BL written in bold type. Emails were sent to confirm receipt but no replies were received. Five days later I rang the reception desk only to discover the folder was never collected. The contact had been a hoax.

After that, such was my mistrust that I almost deleted another offer of assistance. However, feelings of desperation thankfully intervened, and I emailed off the requested documentation in connection with my case to a John Smith. The subsequent emails revealed a man well versed in law as well as the particulars of my own situation that were not included in the emailed documents. For that reason, I believe that John Smith was directly connected to my case.

During the following months John became my ally, legal support and mentor in my fight against injustice. He provided me with legal arguments to use in court as well as writing the affidavit with which I would walk confidently into the Four Courts on 2 April 2012. John also supported my Supreme Court appeal in November 2013 by providing the precedents attached to arguments that would have otherwise cost me hundreds of hours trawling through law books. Sometimes, when I did not understand a point in law, he would explain it in different ways. John was patient with his new student and because of that he was the best teacher I ever had. On occasion I would enquire as to his true identity, but his response was that our collaboration would be discouraged within the legal fraternity, so I didn't press it further. To this day I do not know who John Smith was, but I will always be grateful for his legal counsel and the hope he gave me in my darkest hour.

On the morning of 2 April I walked into court alone. Unable to afford representation, I reminded myself that there were tens of thousands of people in a similar situation throughout Ireland who did not have a John Smith on their side. So, armed with my new arguments and affidavit, I waited for my case number to be called. Scrolling down the list of judges I saw AIB v Darcy – Judge Brian McGovern. The judge who had bankrupted me only months earlier was adjudicating over my case. My heart sank.

It was no secret that Judge McGovern's nickname, Banker's Boy, had been well earned throughout the years due to his concessions to the demands of the banks in whose favour he ruled one hundred per cent of the time. Also in the corner for the bank was Damien West, counsel and envoy for AIB, who, like the king's favourite gladiator, would daily enter the legal arena to fight an opponent who was neither skilled nor versed in the art of legal warfare and for this reason appeared merely to provide entertainment for the gallery.

My case number was called and proceedings began. Damien West opened his case to the court as Judge McGovern noted my lack of counsel and looked at me disapprovingly. He also appeared vexed when the debt of €17.5 million was repeated.

'We have a judgement,' claimed Damien West, without disclosing how it had been obtained.

Then I stood up to read out my affidavit, only to be interrupted by Judge McGovern.

'I've read your affidavit, so carry on,' he said.

I was rooted to the spot. My entire defence had been removed. Attempting to read out another extract, Judge McGovern scolded me.

'I told you that I have read that. Now, do you have anything else to say?'

Damien West sat opposite with a smile as wide as that a Cheshire cat.

'The plaintiff has failed to quantify their loss,' I blurted out, but the judge answered for Damien West.

'Mr Darcy, you got the money. Isn't that the truth?'

'I didn't get any money, Judge. In fact, I got a mortgage-backed security for the plaintiff to generate millions from. It was an unfair and unconscionable contract, which the plaintiff breached.'

Becoming increasingly irritated at my answers, Judge McGovern shouted back, 'You got the money!'

This went on for another few minutes until my patience gave out and I shouted back, 'Judge Elizabeth Dunne ruled that anyone who received a demand letter after 1 December 2009 is prohibited from prosecution. I received the letter of demand on 27 April 2010, which was five months later.'

If Judge McGovern had a morsel of integrity, he would have dismissed the case immediately, but, rather, allowed Damien West's request for an adjournment.

The following week we were back in court listening to the claim that AIB had called in my loans two years earlier, on 30 October 2008. In support of which, a letter was produced claiming to be from AIB that had neither a letterhead nor a signature. I was seething.

'This letter is a fabrication to get around Judge Elizabeth Dunne's ruling,' I said, further explaining that the plaintiff (AIB) had not once in the two years after this alleged letter called in my loans, but had, instead, furnished me with glowing references. I asked for an adjournment to examine my files. Therefore, on 16 April, I walked back into Judge McGovern's court armed with dozens of officially signed letters from AIB testifying to the fact that we were all working together and everything was on track. One letter was even dated 30 October 2008 and was signed by two senior officials in AIB. Another letter, four months later, again confirmed that everything was great. More letters the following year stated the same. There was nothing written from AIB that claimed to call in a loan. 'In which case, this letter is fraudulently produced by Damien West in an attempt to circumvent the Judge Dunne's ruling,' I said.

After reading the letters, Judge McGovern concluded: 'Mr Darcy, I don't just believe you got the letter of demand that called in all the loans on 30 October 2008, I am convinced you got it.'

Realising that this man was going to evict my family, I addressed the court directly:

'Not once did AIB, in the two years after they supposedly called in my loans, mention it. Otherwise, they would have closed off my accounts, which they did not do. Their top officials were writing to me commending my work for the weeks and months after that date and you, Judge McGovern, choose to ignore all the authenticated evidence and believe instead in an unheaded and unsigned letter.'

There was silence in the courtroom. Judge McGovern picked up his gavel. 'I grant the application of the plaintiff and so order possession of Mr Darcy's home.'

Damien West stood up and repeated his mantra.

'Judge, it gives me no pleasure to evict this couple, but my client is out of pocket in this matter.'

I managed to make it outside the courtroom and then collapsed onto the pew with my face in my shaking hands.

'Are you okay?' a voice asked.

I turned around and saw a young man with long black hair and glasses.

'I'm Jerome Reilly.'

He shook my hand and informed me that he was from the press. After sharing my story, he enquired whether I expected sympathy given that I had been a property developer.

'I don't want sympathy,' I replied, 'just information.'

Minutes later a victorious Damien West emerged from court with his entourage congratulating him loudly. Looking up from the pew, our eyes met momentarily.

In turmoil, I walked out of the Four Courts. Adjacent to it was the Bridewell Garda Station where, outside, a prisoner was being escorted into a prison van. It reminded me of my neighbour, Eamonn Lillis, who had killed his wife in the same week as my family's hell had started. I remember thinking that he had had the best of legal counsel, and even in prison all his material needs were met. Yet, like the tens of thousands of families in Ireland facing eviction who had committed no crime, on 16 April my own family paid a price for those who had.

On the bus home panic rose within me. There was no work or the prospect of any, neither was there money or anywhere to go. I sat on a wall outside my estate, listening to my dogs barking and knowing that it was unlikely anyone would take them and they would have to be put down. Clutching my briefcase to shield my face, I sobbed. A neighbour who was passing by asked if I was alright.

'Just bad news,' I replied.

Clare's face met me as I entered my home. I shook my head.

'How long?' she asked.

'Nine months.' I replied.

With our fate apparently sealed, we were woken the following morning with another registered letter from AIB, now demanding the insurance monies from Woodview. The ink was not yet dry on the judge's order and they were already trying to take away any chance we had to start again.

After breakfast I found Clare kneeling over Pisa, crying.

'I can't take this any more,' she said. 'I'd rather be dead than go through this.' I wrapped my arms around her as we leaned into each other and I wondered if there was any fight left in me.

The next Sunday Jerome Reilly's piece on my story appeared in the *Sunday Independent*. Having printed my email address at the end, I was inundated with dozens of messages of sympathy and support from strangers, both domestic and overseas.

John Smith was shocked to hear of the proceedings and continued to help me. Three weeks later I brought a motion to stay Judge McGovern's order of possession of my family home, which would stop the execution of the order. Armed with potentially explosive information from my whistleblowers and arguments supplied by my legal mentor, I once again held in my hands my family's salvation: irrefutable evidence that the letter of 30 October 2008 was a forgery. My new evidence was a letter received from the Revenue Commissioners of Ireland confirming their contact with my bank over VAT (which had subsequently been resolved) at the same time as the forged letter claimed to have been written. This was followed by a letter from the Revenue Commissioners to my bank confirming that everything was perfect with the accounts.

Court 6 was empty. Solicitors for AIB followed me in and Damien West appeared soon after in his new gown and barrister bands. As the registrar called out for silence in court the door opened, and, to my disbelief, Judge Brian McGovern appeared.

Only in Ireland, it seemed, could the same judge adjudicate over an application questioning whether or not his own order should be stayed.

Even before sitting down, Judge McGovern announced to the court.

'Mr Darcy, I don't care what you have to say here today, I have already affirmed my decision.'

'You have predetermined my case before I present it?' I questioned.

'I have already affirmed my decision, Mr Darcy,' he spat back, taking up his gavel and slamming it hard on the mahogany desk in front of him.

I jumped back up, no longer afraid, as the worst had already happened. 'Justice is unobtainable in this court. You haven't heard my case.'

'I have affirmed my decision. You can appeal it to the Supreme Court,' he said coldly. Damien West smiled and said nothing; I had probably made him another €10,000 in fees.

Three weeks later, with my last chance of saving my family from eviction, I brought an application to set aside the judgement that the bank used to get possession, which was based on the fact that I had been unable to attend court on that day due to the trauma of learning of the deaths in my immediate family.

With Mr Justice Seán Ryan (nicknamed the Smiling Mantis) presiding over my case in the High Court, I wondered if my luck had changed. He began by explaining that to set aside a judgement it must be proved that it was by surprise and that it should not have been given. Since my judgement had been obtained in my absence, I had to justify why I did not attend the court on the day.

'Judge, the reason why I didn't attend court was because I had suffered the loss of my home through fire, the collapse of my business and my two brothers and my mother had died. I was unable to function and was suffering from depression, which my doctor will confirm.'

'That's terrible, Mr Darcy,' replied Judge Ryan, 'how are you now?' Taken aback by his concern, I answered that it had been a hard year, at which point he turned to Damien West and asked what the consequences would be were my application to be allowed. My heart raced knowing that, if granted, possession would be impossible to implement.

'Judge, it makes no difference what the outcome is,' Damien West replied. 'I got a possession order for Mr Darcy's property last month so this application is pointless.'

In hindsight, I know that this was simply untrue and just another tactic to mislead the court; however, my ignorance of the law at that time prevented me from contradicting him. Then, for the following forty minutes, counsel for AIB talked about the €17.5 million debt and the lateness of my application, claiming it was a desperate attempt by a desperate man.

Judge Ryan summed up his ruling. 'I sympathise with Mr Darcy for the loss of his home and business, particularly the tragic losses of his brothers and mother and his depression that followed, but I don't think that was reason enough not to have attended court that day.'

Then he picked up his gavel and denied my application. Another €10,000 for Damien West.

Over the next few weeks more whistleblowers came forward, yet their information was not going to save my family. I had appealed Judge McGovern's order to the Supreme Court in the hope that justice might exist in their courtroom, but there had been no word back so far. I had contacted storage companies and Fingal County Council with regards to the possibility of temporary social housing only to be informed that we needed to be already evicted before we would be considered. I also contacted a dog trust who directed me to the local dog pound, which could only hold animals for thirty days, and after which time they would be destroyed. Sitting around the dinner table that Christmas evening 2012, Sabien trotted over and laid his head on my lap. I went out of the room and cried knowing that in four weeks' time, if nobody took them, my dogs would have to be euthanised. The only thing to do was to return to the internet and continue trawling through stories about legal arguments and evictions.

Finally, after another marathon internet search, I came across a report on Seamus Sherlock, an Irish farmer from Limerick, who, having found himself with an order for eviction, barricaded himself into his home for over a year and had thus far prevented an execution of the order due to the requirement for vacant possession. With no other way forward, I decided to use the same tactic and create a barricade at the entrance to my house. I wrapped steel chains around the gates and pushed an old van up against them, ironically with the name of my company that had built 17 and 21 Myra Manor clearly visible along the side. A length of steel was placed across my front door and inside there were secret void spaces to hide; if the sheriff could not get vacant possession, then he could not get my home. All I had to do was stay put.

(In Ireland a sheriff's duties are the same as a bailiff in America.)

However, early that January morning, having run out of milk and estimating that I would be no more than twenty minutes away from home, I grabbed my coat, opened the gates and ran in the direction of the local shops. Assuming that the van parked up the road was connected to one of my neighbours, I thought no more of it.

The fields across to the sea were tipped with snow and I enjoyed my time out of the house and re-engaging with the outside world, if only for a few minutes. On my return, though, my enjoyment left me. As I rounded the corner and my home came into view, I saw four men in dark clothes in my front garden, one of whom was wearing bright orange overalls and was already drilling the front door of my house. Dropping the cartons of milk, I jumped over the wall, passing two security men caught off-guard.

'What are you doing?' I shouted at the man from Dyno-Locks.

'My job,' he replied.

I was now surrounded by six men, the smallest of whom identified himself as the sheriff.

'Can I see your ID,' I asked him, but he turned his back on me as his bodyguards encircled him. I called Dillon on the phone to get help. Looking at strangers invading my home, I was thankful that Clare was visiting her mother at the time.

I stood in the door frame and announced: 'This is private property. You have no legal right to be here.' The sheriff responded that he had an order from the court. However, upon asking him to produce it, the foreign security guards forced me back into the house. Dillon arrived and ran to my side. I instructed him to tell the man from Dyno-Locks to stop drilling the back door of the house, he was immediately confronted by four more ex-army security guards who had joined their colleagues.

At this point the Gardaí arrived. I instructed Dillon not to leave the house, fearing that the security guards would lock the door if they got us out; I walked over to the two Gardaí who were standing outside the perimeter wall of my home. Aware that An Garda Síochána cannot legally enter private property, I invited them in. They stopped at the front door and the sheriff went straight over to them. One of the officers returned to me and said that the sheriff claimed to have a valid order for possession of the property. I asked to see it and his identification. At the same time another patrol car arrived, along with a photographer who parked himself outside the main gate and held up a telescopic lens.

'These papers are not in order,' I informed the Gardaí. The sergeant then took command.

'What's the problem here,' he asked. The sheriff spoke into his ear. Minutes later the sergeant asked, 'What do you say, Mr Darcy, to this claim by the sheriff that he has a court order?'

'It's not valid,' I replied. 'I have a Supreme Court appeal against that order,' which I produced from my bag. The sergeant read the appeal and appeared confused. Turning to me, he repeated the mantra I had heard many times before. 'This is a civil matter, and we are only here to keep the peace.'

Backing away, he joined his uniformed friends. There were now ten security guards and the sheriff in my house, and more of their vans were arriving. Standing at the front door trying to explain my appeal situation to the sergeant, I made the analogy of an inmate on death row waiting for the governor to consider his request for a pardon. They still take him out and execute him but three months later the governor grants him a pardon. The sergeant laughed at the thought.

'I can see what you mean,' he said, but he pretended to take a call on his walkie-talkie and walked away leaving two officers standing at the door. At that moment I heard shouts behind me.

'We'll fuckin' drag you out,' the security men were shouting at Dillon, and they propelled him forward onto the concrete floor.

Crouched over my son's motionless body, panic gripped me. As I looked at his white face lying on the grey floor, the day of his birth flashed before me; he was small enough to cradle in one hand, helpless, a minute old, and I was the proudest man on earth. And now there he was, lying on the floor unconscious, once again helpless, but this time so was I. There was no pride, just humiliation. Mocking laughter echoed from the ceilings of the property being possessed by men. The Gardaí were within touching distance but did not intervene.

'Please God, someone help,' I screamed, but more laughter filled the room.

Frantically checking his temple, I found a large lump. Trying to hold his head above the ice-cold concrete, I managed to get the phone and dialled.

'Ambulance, please, please.' As I was giving the address, Dillon opened his eyes. He was shivering with shock and I begged the tracksuit-clad men to get jackets from the other room, but their replies were deeper tones of laughter. I raced into the other room and gathered all I could carry. Wrapping my son up, I tried to remember the right things to do. The Gardaí, unfazed by events, stood at the entrance door with their eyes focused elsewhere.

'They assaulted my son,' I shouted at them.

'We saw nothing' was their reply.

Then the cruellest act of all: the sheriff, trying to get past my son's body that now blocked the door, walked on Dillon's legs.

'Get off him, you fucking bastard.'

'I'm sorry about that,' he sarcastically replied, to the cackle of his audience.

I looked up from the ground at the two Gardaí and said: 'Did you see him just walk on my son's unconscious body? He just assaulted him again.'

But the answer was the same. 'We didn't see anything.'

Dillon was disorientated and shaking as I drew him into my chest to keep him warm.

'Sorry, didn't see you there,' said the sheriff, as he kneed me in the face on his return. Cue more laughter from the track-suited chorus behind me.

'Jesus Christ, Garda, he just kneed me in the face.' The arrival of the ambulance saved another denial from the corrupt agents of the State. Lying on a stretcher, I watched my son leave but was unable to travel with him because the sheriff would have taken possession. At that moment I lost my sanity. Picking up two scaffolding feet (that is, small hollow steel bars with a steel plate at the end), I demonstrated how to use them to inflict pain.

'Are you threatening the men?' one of the Garda said to me.

'I'm demonstrating to everyone here that if anyone comes near me, I will defend myself.'

Smashing the steel bar through the wooden frame of the door and making the Gardaí jump, I said: 'Call it self-defence.' I then walked into the front room of the house and continued to spin the bars around my shoulders. I then sat down in the corner facing the door. Then everything went quiet. After five minutes I got up and walked to the front door expecting to be rushed, but everyone had gone. I closed the front door and returned to the front room in anticipation of their return.

I stayed there for about an hour and then stood up feeling two feet shorter. With an indescribable fear deep in the pit of my stomach and with my heart pounding, tears welled up. For the people against whom this crime had been perpetrated were not strangers but my own family.

With shallow breaths, I opened the box next to our hall door. Retrieving the brown Abus steel locks and chains that once secured the building site, I walked down the gravel driveway with feelings of humiliation accompanying every step. I wrapped the chains around the metal bars that had been erected by the same hands that now locked my family in like wild animals. With the click of the lock my heart stilled. 'Will the sheriff return tomorrow?' I asked myself. 'Please God, no.'

Momentarily I looked to the sky and asked my late mum and two older brothers for help. 'Good night, Mum, look after them for me,' but the dark sky held no reply. I released the handbrake on the old, red building van and let it freewheel until it stopped, then I pushed it in front of the gate. The wheels turned so slowly that they sank into the gravel. The strength of youth had left me, and I felt my fifty-one years with each step. I was out of breath and exhausted, but the van was in place and the barricade complete.

I walked back through our hall door with fear accompanying every new sound. My mobile made me jump. It was my neighbour Pat from Howth.

'Tom, the sheriff and his men arrived this afternoon and took your home. They have chained the gates and placed a trespass notice on the wall. There's a security van in your driveway.'

I felt overwhelmed. Thanking him for calling, I sat on the stairs alone and cried. Never before did I feel such self-hatred. Clare arrived back two hours later from Beaumont Hospital. Her face was red and her make-up was messed. Pushing back the van and unchaining the gates to let her in, I asked about Dillion. 'They're keeping him in for observation,' she replied, her words trembling as she spoke. I told her about our home in Howth. She placed her head on my shoulder and sobbed uncontrollably.

For the next hour we sat on the floor of 21 Myra Manor cradling each other. A security guard was already sitting in 17 Myra Manor. The sheriff had taken that too. Clare looked up at me, revealing eyes that had cried every night for the last nine months. 'What are we going to do, Tom?' I couldn't reply for I had no answer.

Back in bed staring at the ceiling, I hoped for sleep, but an unfamiliar noise caused my body to jump. It was only my neighbour, returning home late. Looking out the window, I saw a man who did not chain and barricade his home each night. How envious I felt of his life where he can enjoy the simple pleasure of going for a walk without fear that his home could be taken during his absence. At 7 a.m., the bang of a car door under my window caused my stomach to turn with anxiety. Peeping through the curtains I expected to see my family's executioner; someone who holds no thought for the misery they create or fear they instil, but it was just my neighbour's gardener.

My first action of the day was no longer that of a father enjoying breakfast with his family but straight onto social media sites to discover the whereabouts of the sheriff. I checked emails from allies throughout the world and from my two anonymous supporters, who for almost a year had been guiding me in my quest for justice.

It was thirty-nine days since the possession of our home became active. Regardless of what I know about the criminal behaviour of the banks, I cannot stop their thugs from ripping my family from these walls.

'The price for my big mouth', was what one insider from the bank had told me.

What good had it done my family? I wondered, while replying online to some poor unfortunate soul who is beginning the same journey as I am on. A man who has no choice but to pour his heart out to someone he has never met but who understands the humiliation felt at acknowledging the truth of his powerlessness. With each email recounting the same sorry events, my heart grew heavier, for these are just ordinary people going about their lives who have been conditioned to trust their abusers. Every story is the same story except with different names and different solicitors bleeding them dry with warning letters and debt collectors arriving at their door. There is nowhere to turn and no one seems to care. Having attended many funerals of such men, I have seen their children's faces covered in tears as their partner stands over their coffin motionless, and still the vultures circle before the soil can hold the weight of the gravestone not yet paid for. But, according to many of the Coroners' Court, Irish people do not commit suicide; they just accidentally take a dozen rat pellets or throw a rope around a tree and hang themselves.

As a result of watching our home being stripped and sentimental items being sold, arguments between Clare and me had grown more frequent. She had died inside that day, nine months before, when the judge had given possession of our home to the bank. It was the home she had created, nurtured, designed, cared for and loved and where our children had lived and were loved. On 16 April 2012 the judge had sentenced us all to a slow mental death, beginning with the loss of self-respect, then worldly possessions, a happy marriage and finally any sense of normality for our entire family. That same day I had given the interview to Jerome Reilly, and I recounted the loss of my two brothers and my mum, my home and business, all within the same period. I could not have predicted the tsunami of insider information that would follow the article. In fact, such was the impact that two days after its publication I sat in the Burlington Hotel waiting to meet my first whistleblower.

Dressed in tweed, a gentleman approached me and asked if I was Tom Darcy. After surveying the room he seated himself on the edge of an armchair.

'I could lose everything if anyone sees me talking to you,' he whispered. 'You don't know what you're dealing with here.

The banks knew they were insolvent five years ago and kept trading. I have the memos and emails to prove it.' Removing a bundle of papers from his briefcase, he placed them on my open hands.

'Here, take these, I've said enough.' At that point my whistleblower walked quickly out the back entrance of the hotel, hiding his face in an open umbrella and disappeared out of view.

I went straight to the media in the hope of having this information aired but it was not reported, leaving me with no option other than to go back in front of a judge. Combing through folders I came across a civil summons issued by AIB that had spelled my surname incorrectly by using an apostrophe between the letters *d* and *a* in Darcy. So I brought a case under the 'slip rule', which was heard by Ms Justice Elizabeth Dunne. During the proceedings I ensured I introduced my evidence that AIB had failed to perfect their banking licence in accordance with statute law of 1989. When I had completed my presentation, I demanded a judicial review, which I was denied, but Judge Dunne did direct me to go to An Garda Síochána. My intention was to initiate a criminal investigation against this bank.

My appointment was for 2 p.m. the following day at the local Garda station. So armed with the evidence that had been unearthed from my investigations from Government Buildings as well as my prepared statement clipped to the first box, in the early afternoon I walked into the old stone building in the fishing village of Howth.

After twenty minutes I was directed to the interview room, where the community officer, Garda Doyle, sat opposite me. Expecting my visit to be about local planning or the noise pollution of loud music, he asked me what was my concern?

I unclipped my statement and handed it to him. Upon reading the first paragraph, Garda Doyle's eyes opened wider and his eyebrows lifted.

'Jesus, this isn't a planning issue, is it?' he said, without taking his eyes off the statement. Jumping up from his chair, he told me that he would return in a couple of minutes. Such was his haste that the door was left ajar.

'That nutter in there wants us to investigate the banks,' I heard Garda Doyle say to another officer. 'He claims they broke the law. He even lists the laws and has three boxes of evidence.'

'The banks broke the law? 'his colleague replied. 'I think you'd better give someone a call in the Department of Justice.' I smiled to myself.

The next thing I heard was Garda Doyle on the phone to the Department of Justice. 'This is Howth Garda Station,' he said, 'we have a gentleman here who wants to make a criminal allegation against AIB bank. He has three boxes of evidence and a prepared statement.' At which point, Garda Doyle read out the statement, listened to the reply and hung up. About forty minutes later he reappeared through the door.

'I'm sorry, Mr Darcy, we can't take your statement.' 'Why not?' I asked. 'This is beyond my pay grade; look I just can't take this.'

Aware that some years earlier at the same Garda Station an investigation had been conducted after a statement had been received from a young man (who was intoxicated) regarding a flying saucer that he claimed to have seen over Howth Head, I challenged Garda Doyle directly.

'You can accept a report of a UFO, but not a criminal allegation against a bank?' Garda Doyle bent down to pick up my boxes. 'I'm sorry Mr Darcy, I'll show you out.'

After the boxes had been packed into my car, Garda Doyle turned to me. 'Off the record,' he whispered, 'do you understand the consequences of what you're trying to do?' 'I do,' I answered. 'I want those who broke our laws to be held accountable.' At which point he looked me straight in the face. 'That will never happen, Mr Darcy, you're fooling yourself.'

During the next few days I contacted a further six Garda Stations in Dublin but each one refused to give me an appointment. It seemed that word had got around of my visit and now I was virtually barred from Garda Stations. After three weeks I called Niall Boylan who was a host on one of Dublin's radio stations. Finding my story difficult to believe, his scepticism soon turned to anger when he rang a Garda Station and tried to make an appointment. However, at the mention of my name, the Garda at the other end hung up. So in his capacity as an investigative journalist, Niall rang the Garda Press Office to complain and two days later the secretary for the superintendent from Coolock Garda Station offered to take my statement.

I chose to give my statement at Malahide station at 9 p.m. the following evening because it closes at 7 p.m. and I wanted to see how urgent my complaint was being taken. At 8.55 p.m. armed with my boxes and statement, I rang the doorbell. The same sergeant who had attended my own eviction opened the door.

'Mr Darcy, we've being expecting you,' he said. It took thirty minutes to give my statement, after which I asked when I could expect to receive the PULSE number, which is the computer-generated number allocated to the crime/incident in the Garda computer system, but the sergeant shook his head.

'I've done what was asked of me here; the rest is up to the top brass,' he said and closed the door behind me. Five days later I phoned Malahide Garda station to say that I hadn't received the PULSE number but I got the same response. 'I've done what was asked off me, Mr Darcy; the rest is up to the top brass.'

Over the next couple of weeks I sent out press statements informing the media of the criminal allegation I had made against AIB and the unusual procedure I had to go through to get the police to take my statement, coupled with the fact that no PULSE number had been issued, but not one reply was received. Dillon, my son, sensing my frustration, suggested that I encourage my Facebook friends to take my statement and include their own personal details and submit it to their local Garda station. For two months each day dozens of Facebook friends private messaged me to confirm that they had submitted their statement, so that by the last week in April virtually every county in Ireland was represented in this national criminal investigation against all the Irish banks until finally on 5 May 2013 I received my PULSE number, a vital component needed for the next stage of my plan.

Given that the Irish police are connected to police forces throughout the world, I contacted each of them directly to inform them of this investigation. I notified Ameripol, Interpol, the FBI, Cyberpol, Europol, the European Central Bank (ECB), International Monetary Fund (IMF), the European Parliament, the Banking Regulation and Supervision Agency asking them to investigate the actions of Irish banks who had broken European laws. I included supporting evidence of insolvency and liquidity violations and a copy of my statement to the Irish police with confirmation of the investigation. I have not received one letter, email or phone call from the Gardaí, the Garda Ombudsman or anyone in the Irish media.

Unfortunately, all my potential 'helpers' were not always so helpful. Vilified in the media, property developers became pariahs overnight, and as such many became targets. Denis Finn, a developer from Howth, was one of the first to feel the wrath of a censored media. Consistently depicted as leading a grandiose lifestyle detached from ordinary life, the truth was that Denis had worked for over forty years building up his business. He was a generous and thoughtful man whose mistake, like the rest of us, was trusting corrupt banking institutions.

I, too, was to feel the wrath of this propaganda, when, soon after meeting my first whistleblower, I arranged to meet a persistent emailer who claimed to offer information about the head of AIB. I had just placed my hand on the old, heavy entrance door of the designated hotel when a guy with a shaved head and bulging shiny suit kicked the door at me, catching my shoulder and propelling me to the ground.

'Fucking property scumbag. You caused all this shit,' he shouted.

Raising his foot over me, I grabbed it, pushed it up and brought him crashing to the ground. Now standing, I placed my foot on his neck and pressed as hard as my fourteen stone would allow, threatening to snap his collarbone. After a few moments, I released him and he scurried away.

It was a few days later, while scanning the hundreds of emails received when I came across an email entitled Ciutu. Intrigued, I opened it and found an attachment containing a memo from one of Ireland's banks. Within the body of the memo was acknowledgement that they could not legally renew their banking licence. Given the format and absence of spelling mistakes, it appeared that the author was well versed in sending professional emails, and, following her direction, I googled the Central Bank of Ireland statute laws and printed the twenty-one page banking application form. I had found the Holy Grail that could irrefutably prove that the banks of Ireland had committed criminal acts.

3

My Supreme Court Win

The Supreme Court appeal was our final attempt to stop AIB from taking possession of our family home. If they succeeded, we would be homeless, and, given our age, it was unlikely that Clare and I would find gainful employment easily. We were no longer the young couple who had dusted themselves off and started their lives over again but were now middle-aged and exhausted from the stress of court appearances and the prospect of feeling the sharp edge of Damocles' sword.

Given the strength of our arguments and the evidence presented leading up to the Supreme Court, on 13 November 2013 it appeared that justice had been done. We proved that Clare had not signed the declaration of consent (or family home consent), nor had she given consent, and therefore our home was protected under the Family Home Protection Act 1976. As a result, a possession from the bank should be unobtainable.

In hindsight, however, it seemed that our victory had less to do with the evidence presented by us to the court and more to do with the potential consequences for the bank, should our arguments be made public. What follows is an extract from these arguments against the bank's legal counsel who was trying to prove that Clare had signed the documents required and that the bank did not need her signature, now claiming that it was a commercial loan, even though they knew that Clare and I were living in our family home, Woodview, in

Howth, prior to any signing, and so by law they required her signature of consent.

Court script:

Tom Darcy begins his defence: 'The plaintiff (AIB) has not presented to this honourable court a signed declaration of consent to the mortgage of Mrs Darcy's family home, Woodview, which is required by law under the Family Home Protection Act of 1976. What the plaintiff has produced is their own replying affidavit of Mr Kevin Daly of 2 May 2013, as exhibited in KL3, which is an undated letter signed by a trainee solicitor from the office of Marcus Lennon Solicitors stating that Woodview was not, nor has ever been, the family home. This letter is from a person who has neither met nor spoken with Mrs Darcy and who, according to the Law Society of Ireland, only commenced employment at the offices of Marcus Lennon Solicitors three months after the mortgage document was allegedly signed.* [The Law Society of Ireland keeps records of all staff in solicitors' offices throughout Ireland when they start and finish employment.] *Mrs Darcy never returned to Marcus Lennon's office after 27 January 2006, as the diaries of Marcus Lennon's office reflect, so this letter is a lie and a fabrication. Furthermore, there is no doubt that the staff from the AIB Sutton branch, who visited Mrs Darcy and her family celebrating their first Christmas in Woodview, Grey's Lane, in 2005, did so prior to the signing of any documents. They were all aware that Mrs Darcy and her family were living in Woodview and that it was the family home, as evidenced in exhibit AD3, which showed bank statements from AIB identifying the address of Mrs Darcy as Woodview, Grey's Lane, in the month of November 2005.* [I further presented electricity bills from October 2005 and gas bills from October 2005.] *However, nowhere in the mortgage document did it mention Mrs Darcy's family home, Woodview, by name or address. Mrs Darcy did not give her prior* consent to the mortgage of her family home, Woodview. Mrs Darcy did not give her informed consent to the mortgage of her family home, and Mrs Darcy did not get independent legal advice'.

[I then cited the Supreme Court ruling of Smyth v the Bank of Ireland 1995.]

'The plaintiff has not presented to this honourable court a declaration of consent to the mortgage of Mrs Darcy's family home, Woodview, which is required to be signed by Mrs Darcy by law and which is also a requirement under the Family Home Protection Act of 1976. The plaintiff cannot argue that it didn't require such declarations when the plaintiff produced two questionable, contradictory declarations for buildings that were not built at that time. They didn't exist. This was intended to confuse and mislead this court.'

[I knew the Central Statistics Office showed that there were over 1.3 million married women in Ireland, and under the Family Home Protection Act 1976 every one of them is required to sign consent when mortgaging their home.] 'If this court is saying, because they are registered on the title deeds [husband's and wife's name on title], that the bank does not need consent when a legal form exists for that purpose, then this court would be stating that cohabiting couples and same-sex couples have superior rights than married couples because they are not registered on title, which I find contradictory to the Constitution of Ireland. Under Article 41.1, the state promises to 'protect the family' and recognises the family as having 'inalienable and imprescriptible rights, antecedent and superior to all positive law'. What superior rights exist when documents required by law to be signed are ignored in favour of banks? Furthermore, this would mean that even if half of the 1.3 million married women in Ireland did not consent to the mortgage of their home, nor receive independent legal advice or sign mandatory required documentation, then their mortgages could be null and void. Multiplying 650,000 people by an average house *price of €300,000 that would cost the Irish banks €195 billion in void mortgages.'*

At that point, the three judges stood up and said that they needed to deliberate. Twenty minutes later they returned.

'Mr Darcy, the issues you raise have such national importance that we consider you should seek a new beginning, if you know what I mean.' New Beginnings was a group of barristers who had formed the previous year to provide legal representation to people in danger of losing their homes. My response to the bench was that I could not afford a barrister.

'You won't have any problem getting a barrister in this room,' one of the judges assured me. The case was adjourned until 13 November 2013. News had already reached Ross Maguire, senior counsel attached to New Beginnings, of the events in the Supreme Court, and it was agreed that he would represent Clare and that I would remain a lay litigant in person.

Soon the 13 November had arrived. This was the forty-seventh time we appeared in court and with not a single win behind us, the anxiety between Clare and me was palpable. Should the Supreme Court refuse my appeal, we would be homeless.

Walking into the Supreme Court at 10.30 a.m., I looked at the solicitors for the bank. It was just another day's work to them that would increase their bulging bank accounts. Seated in their midst was Damien West.

'It doesn't give me any pleasure in evicting this couple,' he had repeated to the court many times, while using every legal route to ensure that this is exactly what would happen.

Such was my mistrust of the Irish legal fraternity that I wondered if the advice given months earlier by the Supreme Court had been an attempt to sabotage my defence, so in light of this possibility I had paid a junior barrister to attend in my place. Although unfamiliar with the facts, he would none-theless add another reason to seek an appeal to the European Court of Human Rights should this hearing go pear-shaped.

The three judges walked out and took their seats. Representing Clare, Ross Maguire opened by listing the long history of the case and then focused on the letter of 30 October 2008 that was unsigned and unheaded, the same letter that Judge McGovern was convinced I had received. As Ross Maguire sat down, my own barrister informed the court of his recent appointment and then proceeded to list some points I had already raised in the original case before Judge McGovern. After five minutes he sat down, at which point Ross Maguire made his apologies to the court and left, citing another case that needed attention. Damien West then stood for over forty minutes and explained the same reasons for proceeding for the possession of my home, as he had in the previous forty-six hearings against me.

Now past 1 p.m. the court adjourned for lunch.

Clare and I left the room, and outside Vincent Martin, a junior barrister, commented that he thought it had gone well. Finding a quiet corner in a local pub, we sat in silence over a coffee. If the verdict went against us, we had no money for a deposit to rent a house. It was like a slow death that felt overwhelming. By 1.55 p.m. we were standing outside the courtroom. Accompanying us in, Vincent tried to be upbeat.

'Okay folks, we still have a fighting chance.'

On the opposite side there again was Damien West looking confident of his forty-seventh knockout. As the judges appeared and went slowly through the points of the case, each statement appeared to confirm the bank's position more strongly. Then the question of the demand letter of 30 October 2008 was raised, and as Ms Justice Mary Laffoy agreed that it did not exist, my heart exploded from within. I turned to Clare and squeezed her hand.

'We've won,' I whispered.

Glancing across the room, I could see Damien West shifting in his seat and biting his lower lip. Stretching forward, he was clearly seething.

Then the judge said, 'We find the order of Judge McGovern unlawful and set aside his order giving an order of all costs to the Darcys.'

True to form, Damien West sprung up and argued that his client AIB had a judgement against us for €17.5 million and demanded that the case be returned back to the chancery list for a plenary hearing (which is a full hearing of all the arguments), as well as the costs to be stayed. The court denied his request for costs but granted the plenary hearing, and for the second time in three years I witnessed Damien West lose his composure and storm out of the courtroom.

'Great news for you both, I'm sure,' congratulated Vincent, 'a great victory.' Having known and worked with Vincent over the years, I can say that he is one of the few decent men who acts with integrity within the Four Courts and I was delighted to have had him with us on that occasion.

After they left, Clare and I instinctively held each other and then phoned the boys. The next morning I was shocked to be awoken by the sound of the doorbell. Assuming it to be the sheriff, I peered out from behind the curtains, but it was the bank's agent who had arrived with a large brown bag with the keys to my properties. Feeling like I was floating on air, I knew that I had accomplished the impossible.

Although we had won our Supreme Court appeal, the fact that it had not been achieved on a point in law (which would have been that Woodview was the family home and that the bank should have obtained Clare's signature rather than that the letter produced by Damien West was fraudulent) meant that AIB could continue their pursuit of me. Conversely, had we won on this point of law, then Irish banks would have been left with hundreds of billions of euro in void mortgages, which our indebted judiciary would never have allowed. Therefore, our Supreme Court win appeared to have had less to do with the fictitious letter and more to do with the unconscionable consequences for Irish banks should the truth have been brought to the European courts. So, far from being stopped in his tracks, Damien West was all fired up and getting ready for his third set of proceedings against me.

The first set of proceedings had been initiated after 27 April 2010 (ref. no. 2010/539SP), and over the next three years Damien West had gone through forty-six different courts until the Supreme Court ruled that the court order for the eviction of my family was unlawful. After standing for forty minutes and arguing his case, a plenary hearing was granted, which allowed the initiation of a second set of proceedings with the same case number. However, Damien West quickly realised that this second set of proceedings would be based on the Land and Conveyancing Law Reform Act 2009, upon which the first set of proceedings had been based, only this time he had no fraudulent letter around which to circumvent Judge Dunne's ruling.

Now realising that the case was unwinnable, Damien West began his third set of proceedings, and so on 21 November 2013, eight days after the Supreme Court ruling, I received my second demand letter. This was followed in January 2014 by new proceedings against me (ref. no. 2014/44SP), which were almost the same as the first set of proceedings (ref. no. 2010/539SP), the only difference being that the figure had jumped from €17.5 million to €21 million (due to the overcharging/theft of €2 million interest), and, of course, it was with reference to the Land and Conveyancing Law Reform Act 2013. Unlike the Land and Conveyancing Law Reform

Act 2009, the 2013 Act does not entitle the homeowner to a full hearing, only to a summary summons, which is contrary to our Constitution. Now Damien West could fast-track the possession of my home. For these proceedings I was given a court date of 16 May 2014 for a hearing in the Master's Court.

In a separate case, I was in court on 4 April 2014 regarding the insurance monies. During the hearing, Ms Justice Mary Laffoy (who had presided over the Supreme Court hearing in November 2013) enquired as to 'the situation with the other case' (ref. no. 2010/539SP), which she assumed had been returned to plenary hearing. When the court was informed that there were now two sets of identical proceedings running in tandem that were contrary to the Rules of the Superior Courts, Noel Gillespie, counsel for AIB, was asked if he knew anything about it.

Although he fervently denied knowledge of any such proceedings, I did not trust him. For less than nine months earlier Noel Gillespie had stated in open court that 'if the Darcys won their Supreme Court appeal, the insurance monies for the rebuild of their home would be theirs'. To this day, AIB has refused to honour their court order and the insurance monies remain locked in a bank account, whilst the first floor rebuild of Woodview has become so battered by four consecutive winters that it will have to be torn down and rebuilt. We are still displaced from our home and continue to live in the half-built house of 21 Myra Manor.

After the weekend, on 9 April, I received a notice of discontinuance of the case number 2010/539SP. Upon hearing of the story of the second set of proceedings now being pursued against me by the bank (ref. no. 2014/44SP), on 16 May an international barrister specialising in banking corruption attended court on my behalf, where he was met with a hostile reception from Damien West, who went so far as to question his professional credentials. Twenty minutes later the master the High Court dismissed the bank's case, and for the first time in five years I had no proceedings against me. It seemed that international representation might be the way to go. However, not fifteen minutes later, Damien West was in Court 3, where the property investor and judge, Mr Justice Paul Gilligan granted him leave by way of an ex parte application (without the knowledge of the other party), to appeal the master's decision. Ironically, this is something that Judge Gilligan, in my five years' experience in his court, never gave to defendants. It is worth noting that on that date Judge Gilligan had property investments that were financed by numerous banks, which he never declared.

'I have absolutely no sympathy for the Darcys,' Judge Gilligan had publicly stated. 'They haven't paid back one penny to the banks in five years.'

He was unwilling to hear that AIB had been offered the full market value of my entire building portfolio (as valued by one of AIB's own approved property valuers) from an independent investor who wanted to buy it. After all, that was all AIB was ever likely to get, the open market value, which was worth far less to them now because of the wasted millions in legal fees.

In light of Judge Gilligan's comment, which I claimed was prejudiced and biased, the case was referred to Mr Justice David Keane, who ruled in favour of Damien West (surprise!), thereby granting him possession. That is where I find myself now, as we go to print, appealing the decision of Judge Gilligan in overturning the master's decision, which will be heard in 2016 in the Court of Appeal. At the same time, I am appealing Judge Keane's decision, arguing that the case should never have been heard. I served AIB and Paul Cody with a counterclaim for deceit and conspiracy and issued a motion seeking the payment of insurance monies to enable me to rebuild our home.

Because of the stress endured by my family during those years, we were looking forward to having our awarded costs being paid, as we had no money nor any belongings left to sell. We were even hoping to go for a short holiday. Sadly our optimism was short-lived because to this day we have not received a euro of the costs awarded to us. Unlike Seán FitzPatrick, disgraced former chairman of Anglo Irish Bank, who, after winning his case and costs, when the latter was not forthcoming quickly enough, claimed that he was unable to proceed effectively with his defence against the opposition's appeal, and for this reason his constitutional rights were being violated. The court agreed, and regardless of his confession of manipulating share values and loan book entries, Seán FitzPatrick received his costs immediately. Yet, two years after being awarded costs by the highest court in the land, we still have received nothing from a bank that writes its own rules and which are endorsed by Irish judges.

Having been assured by various contacts within the media prior to the Supreme Court win that a successful outcome would be reported, the letter below was received by most Irish editors, though not one response was received.

15 November 2013
To the Editor,
On 13 November 2013 I became the first person in Ireland as a lay litigant in person to win in the Supreme Court after being evicted from my home. It resulted in the return of my family home, the same one I was evicted from originally.

I initiated a criminal investigation against all banks in Ireland on 14 February 2013: Pulse No (FB11.117.13) issued by An Garda Síochána, copy of statement attached. This investigation into banking corruption is the first in Irish history and the first in European history.

I am one of the founding members of the New Land League
of Ireland (NLLI) fighting against evictions of innocent
families throughout Ireland and the horrific increased suicide
rate that is a direct result of the actions of Irish banks. The
NLLI actions have forced auctioneers to withdraw and to stop
selling or offering family homes or businesses, in some cases
resulting in contractual agreements with the same auctioneers,
reference Alsop's Auctioneers 4th July 2013.
Regards,
Tom Darcy

On 2 July 2013, I received an email from a couple whose
possessed home was being auctioned off by Allsop in Dublin.
Allsop was an English auctioneering house franchised out to
Irish agents. Their chosen venue was not without irony
because the Shelbourne Hotel had been the location of the
drafting of the Irish Constitution from February to May 1922.
It is a place where bullets had flown, bombs had exploded and
the Irish had risen up against their oppressor. Now, less than
a century later, the English were once again benefiting from
the evicted Irish, not with the assistance of the Black and Tans
but with our own who had forsaken their history in favour of
euro and bonds.

My plan was to bring awareness to the plight of homeless
families across the country. Jerry Beades, whom I had known
since my property developing days, having had dealings with
the banks himself, was more than happy to be involved. In
fact, such was his enthusiasm that he had plastered the words
of Charles Stewart Parnell's speech denouncing evictions
around his restored vintage truck.

'When a man takes a farm from which another had been
evicted you must shun him on the roadside when you meet
him, you must shun him in the streets of the town, you must

shun him in the shop, you must shun him in the fair green and in the marketplace, and even in the place of worship, by leaving him alone, by putting him in a moral Coventry, by isolating him from the rest of his country as if he were the leper of old, you must show your detestation of the crime he has committed.'

So with our plan hatched, I posted for support on my Facebook page, which was the first time I had used the social media site for this reason, hoping that 350 or at least 200 people would attend the auction with us.

The morning of the auction, Jerry parked his truck outside the former Anglo Irish Bank building, a befitting place to promote the injustice of evictions. PA systems were mounted and a couple of hundred flyers had been printed. Posters depicting the Toiseach Enda Kenny as a traitor were also made visible. By 9 a.m., we were the only ones standing. I had drafted a four-page statement identifying the C1 charges registered in the company's office and proving that all Irish banks had been insolvent since February 2008, as well as the fact that An Garda Síochána had failed to launch a national criminal investigation into the banks of Ireland.

As the prospective buyers began to arrive, Jerry continued to hand out flyers.

'Please don't buy a family's home,' he called out, as they looked at each other with bemusement at the apparent absurdity of such a request. By 10.30 a.m., we were a total of eight. Sensing my disappointment, Jerry turned to me smiling. 'Let's go in and embarrass the parasites.'

Walking up the centre aisle, we recognised familiar faces who had come to witness their homes being sold for a tenth of the price they had paid, knowing that they would be pursued for the residual debt. The top table was draped in red, perhaps symbolising the blood of our patriots along with those who stood with them and now the lives of those who could no longer take the pain. With Lot 1 about to go under the hammer, Jerry stood up and started quoting Charles Stewart Parnell. Staring at those who avoided his gaze, a young couple then asked the room not to buy their family home as they were now homeless with their two children. Clare Leonard, one of our group, stood up and said that the titles were not given in good faith, while I walked to the back the room awaiting the imminent arrival of An Garda Síochána.

On cue, a superintendent and six Gardaí arrived.

'This is a peaceful demonstration,' I assured him, 'we're here to inform the room of the issues attached to the homes being sold here today.'

I had pressed Jerry's number on my mobile so he knew the Gardaí were present, at which point support arrived and swelled our numbers to over two dozen. Meanwhile, Jerry continued to rhyme off Parnell's speech with such passion that Parnell himself would have been proud!

The top table, aghast at the spectacle of Jerry, the Gardaí and the commotion at the back of the room, huddled together with hotel management.

'It's a peaceful demonstration; we are not breaking any laws,' I continued. At that point, more people stood up and addressed those seated on either side of them, telling how their children sleep in friends' houses while they spend the night in cars and derelict buildings. Embarrassed, people started to leave, scurrying through the exit doors holding their hands up to shield their faces.

I glanced across the room as the auction was officially cancelled. Returning Jerry's smile with a thumbs up, we felt satisfied at having halted the fire sale of Irish homes. Outside the journalists were waiting. Speaking to Valerie Cox of RTÉ, I produced the C1 mortgage document from the Companies

Registration Office proving the insolvency of our banks since 2008 and resulting in all mortgages taken out after that year being rendered invalid. However, rather than highlighting the illegality of the banks' position, the media focused on my mistaken reference to Constance Markievicz as a man, a slip of the tongue that in no way warranted the attention that it received. Instead, all attention should have been placed firmly at the doors of our financial institutions and their criminal behaviour. In fact, such was the backlash against my exposure of the banks, that the said clip was uploaded to YouTube. It appeared that everyone had been well and truly hoodwinked, though much to my delight, the following morning the same clip had received over sixty thousand views. My gaff, it appeared, now had people asking about the day's events.

Emerging from the Shelbourne Hotel, Jerry and I felt like we were standing in the shoes of the men who, one hundred and twenty-five years earlier, had fought similar tyranny and injustice. Asked by a reporter if we considered ourselves to be the successors of the Land League of Parnell and Davitt, we replied that we had stopped families' homes being sold there that morning, which was what we intended to do. However, unintentional as it was, our rebirth of the Land League of Ireland was the result of our early morning raid on 4 July in the Shelbourne Hotel, where Ireland's 1 per cent had gathered to feast on a banquet of heartache and forced poverty upon a nation.

Still enjoying our achievement, two days later I received a letter from AIB informing me they were selling my home Woodview as well as the Waterside development land, even though Damien West had never sought an order of sale from the court. So legally they couldn't sell my home or my site. The following week Ganly Walters Auctioneers placed three-metre red square signs in the front garden of our home and advertised the sale on their website. Waterside was now reduced from €10 million to €800,000, which was 10 cent on the euro and 17 Myra Manor was going for €400,000 from €3.5 million. In total my building portfolio had been reduced from €17.5 million to €1.4 million. By the second weekend in August 2013, my whistleblower told me that viewings had been arranged. So I got my Facebook friends to contact the owner of Ganly Walters asking him not to sell in light of the legal requirements and litigation attached to the property. They phoned him at all hours of the day and night and bombarded him with emails.

That year, my birthday was celebrated standing outside my family home holding a placard asking strangers not to buy my home. A dozen Facebook friends, including Dillon's former babysitter who I hadn't seen for years, arrived to give support, handing out flyers to those seeking to benefit from the fire sale of my home. Not surprisingly An Garda Síochána arrived within minutes. The same Garda, who had refused to take my criminal statement, was now intent on protecting the agents of the same criminal bank. The events that day deterred potential buyers.

Given that the charade that morning had stemmed from the return of eviction to Ireland, it appeared that the only way to put a permanent halt to the destruction of families was to take a constitutional challenge against the Land and Conveyancing Law Reform Act 2013. Having already been pursued under the Land and Conveyancing Law Reform Act 2009, I had thus far been prevented from taking such a challenge, but having won my case I was now in a position to do so.

To every newspaper editor in Ireland, the Irish media have, throughout these three years, remained muted in exposing or reporting the truth of these matters. One of the twenty-eight parliamentary questions I proposed was finally answered by the Minister for Finance, Michael Noonan, in January 2013. 'Did the IBRC have a banking licence prior to liquidation?' Pearse Doherty of Sinn Féin asked, to which Minister Noonan answered, 'No'. That is an admission of criminal action (Central Bank Act of 1989) by the bank and yet it never received an inch of ink in any Irish newspaper.

I also brought an interlocutory injunction against the President of Ireland for signing the Land and Conveyancing Law Reform Bill 2013 ("Eviction Bill') hoping it would cause him to refer it to the Council of State.

I also initiated a name-and-shame campaign against the ninety TDs (Members of Parliament) who voted in favour of the Eviction Bill – the same TDs who would stand outside their constituents' homes in solidarity when they were being evicted and say, 'It's immoral to evict a family'. Some even sat on boards and groups that assist homeless families.

The hypocrisy and censorship that exist in Ireland erodes our democracy. I respectfully ask on behalf of the NLLI and all who suffer at the hands of corrupt banking institutions for you or your colleagues to open and expose this Pandora's box, thus far nailed shut by our government and media.

I write this after being told of another father who took his own life, another family destroyed and more childhoods desecrated.

I implore you to report the true price innocent families across Ireland are paying for the criminal actions of corrupt banks.

Regards,

Tom Darcy

Unsurprisingly, it was on the international forum during the summer of 2013 that my case got the most attention. Such was the disbelief of some forum members that I was accused of fabricating the story. The following month, however, I spoke at a rally against eviction outside Government Buildings. Earlier that day, I had stood in another church as a family buried their loved one. Not realising the toll these lost lives were having on me emotionally, I tried to focus on my speech, but the microphone shook in my hand. There were hundreds of people present but no media to report on the truth of what was happening in their own country – only to misinterpret the anger of distressed people as a violent rabble out to create disorder.

I began by outlining the criminal acts that had been committed against the Irish people by our own banks. This was followed by the announcement of an investigation by An Garda Síochána into the same banks, which having been insolvent since February 2008 had subsequently continued to trade illegally. I ended my speech by predicting that my words would go unreported, which was proved right the following day with no mention of it in the media. On a more positive note, after hearing my public statement, Brian Reilly, a neighbour whom I had never met before, invited me to meet him for coffee. Brian was to become a good friend and support in my life, and during the following months helped me move my ambitions forward. Firstly, I would run as a Member of the European Parliament (MEP) candidate, during which time I would be guaranteed at least two interviews on national television; the media could not deny me that.

A few weeks later my campaign got underway. With the help of my sons, I put up posters and, together with the New Land League truck kindly donated by founder Jerry Beades, we were off. My first interview was on TV3 with broadcaster Vincent Browne. Seated next to Brian Hayes, Fine Gael TD, I turned to him and asked why he had voted to evict families. He denied doing any such thing and then broadcaster Vincent

Browne ignorantly shouted over me when I spoke of the banking corruption and the criminal investigation. Finally, upon raising the issue of securitisation and the selling of loans, in light of the admission on the Anglo Tapes about the securitisation of €6 billion, I asked why no TD, economist or broadcaster had addressed it, but Vincent Browne quickly repudiated my statement claiming never to have heard of such a thing. The next day I sent him and his researchers a transcript of the Anglo-Irish tapes, highlighting the passage that proved my claim. I never received an apology or a return invitation to TV3.

It must be noted that TV3 received write-offs from its debts of €140 million held by Irish Bank Resolution Corporation (IBRC). Does that influence their reporting? You be the judge of that!

The following night I was on RTÉ's *Prime Time* where the candidates were split into two groups. The first were comprised of the well-funded candidates from Government. While the second group were candidates who did not have a limitless supply of taxpayers' money at their disposal. The host, David McCullagh began by focusing on my career as a developer with reference to the registered amount of money I allegedly owed.

'Tom, you are a former developer who owes €17.5 million.' My reply was unexpected.

'Just like every viewer at home, I broke no laws and committed no crimes. I trusted a regulated entity that itself broke the laws of this country.'

He quickly replied, 'Tom, you owe €17.5 million'. I then asked David that had he been told the truth when he and thousands of other borrowers signed up with the banks, that these same banks were insolvent, bankrupt and trading with no licence, would he have entered into an agreement with them. He replied that he would not have. I went on to inform him of the criminal investigation against the banks by An Garda Síochána. Again, he attempted to dismiss this fact.

During the following weeks I received great support from people who felt voiceless and abandoned by their public representatives. Then, one Saturday afternoon, while driving my little vintage truck around Dublin city centre, I parked on Saint Stephen's Green where a new supportive friend came into my life. Assuming the knock on my window to be another questioning member of the electorate, it was only when she referred to my call for support on Facebook did I realise that she was offering to help me as a canvasser.

'Hi Tom, I'm Gemma,' the young woman said as she opened the door. 'I read on Facebook that you need help.'

This was a plea I had repeated each day with little or no response and was genuinely surprised that someone would surrender their Saturday afternoon to give out flyers and sit in an old truck with a stranger. Inviting her to jump in, my shield of cynical belief in humanity was finally fractured. Soon we were enjoying each other's conversation. An accomplished author and editor, Gemma showed a genuine interest in my stories of a past life and a book I had once written. Locked away in a briefcase stored in the shed, it had been twenty years since I had opened it. Chronicling my days as a taxi driver in the 1980s, it detailed my founding of the National Taxi Drivers Union of Ireland and how subsequent threats against my family culminated in my young son being handed an empty bottle of sulphuric acid. Gemma and I spoke at length about many ideas and possibilities and eventually decided that I would write this book and she would edit it. We agreed that given the media's stance of 'the blind eye and the deaf ear', an independently published book would be the only way that the truth would emerge about the unholy alliance between the government, the legal fraternity and the banking sector.

It was polling day, 23 May 2014 for the local and European elections. At the counting centre in the RDS, the main candidates strutted around confidently. After raiding the depleting resources of the taxpayers' coffers, the same men and women who had signed to evict families from their homes arrived in State cars and were ushered around like film stars. The tally counters from each of the political parties included dozens of volunteers fighting for any vote that might be considered spoiled. Standing alone, I envied their support as my feeble attempt with two hundred and fifty flyers and posters became embarrassingly obvious. Preparing for a shameful defeat, by midnight the first count had been delivered and I was safe. Only an hour later, on the second round, was I eliminated. So, with seven thousand votes attached to my name, I walked out of the RDS with my head held high.

Having achieved more than expected, I now focused on my dream of creating an international legal seminar with the barristers I had befriended on forums throughout the world. Together we would discuss the implications of a biased legal system, and with their combined expertise we would provide support to Irish litigants. As a result, Brian Reilly and I founded Legal & Equitable, a non-profit agency that continues to introduce those in need of legal advice to our international teams.

On the morning of 8 June 2014, I walked into the Innovation Campus in Dublin City University, Glasnevin, in anticipation of the first seminar on banking corruption in Ireland. The media no-show came as no surprise, but I was too excited by my impending visitors to care.

As sound engineers made last-minute adjustments, a taxi pulled up outside. With his refined English accent, Godfrey was first out of the car followed by Hans, whose tall, sporty build was far removed from the banker stereotype. With over twenty-eight years in banking, treasury and securities, Hans would have much to offer our group. Then there was Al from New York: in his late sixties, with grey hair, silver-rimmed glasses and a deep Italian–American accent, he looked straight at me.

Do you know this guy, Tom Darcy?' he asked, smiling.

'Tom, we finally meet.' said Hans. Godfrey was next to shake my hand, at which point the second taxi pulled up. Trevor, our securitisation specialist, stepped out, followed by Alastair, our barrister from Scotland, and Rebecca, our forensic accountant and interest fraud specialist from Brussels. After more greetings we went into the auditorium where they were introduced to Brian. The itinerary for the day was that I would speak first, which would be followed by questions and answers, and then there would be private sessions where potential clients could have their cases reviewed.

By 3 p.m., the top table were in disbelief at the stories being discussed: mis-selling of products, manipulation of interest and violations of EU regulations. Case after case, true stories of criminal negligence were recounted. Former head of treasury and securities with HSBC, Barclays and RBS banks, Godfrey recounted a story that I had told him months previously, which had become the impetus for his attendance at our Legal & Equitable Seminar.

'Tom told us about an elderly man in his seventies,' Godfrey began, 'who found himself in the High Court in 2012. Pursued by Arthur Cox Solicitors on behalf of First Active bank, ten years earlier, the same man had been represented by Arthur Cox when his late wife had died in a car accident. Now First Active was suing this man for breach of contract regarding a property, but they needed to prove that both his and his wife's names were on the contract, so into evidence they produced a contract that showed his wife's signature, only it had been drafted seven years after she died. At which point, her death certificate was produced, thereby rendering it impossible that his wife could have signed the contract. However, in a bizarre twist, the judge, in his wisdom concluded that he thought it possible and ruled in favour of the bank.'

Godfrey continued.

'It was only when Tom provided us with the evidence of this case that we realised how corrupt Ireland actually is, and this is the reason why we are here today.'

He further explained that none of the legal professionals at the top table had any affiliation with banks; in fact, they only fought against the banks and, in turn, listed their successful cases. They then voiced their unanimous disbelief at the 100 per cent success rate of the banks in Ireland against defendants, with myself being an exception. However, in light of the fact that the Irish legal fraternity receive 90 percent of their revenue from the same banks, this outcome is far from surprising.

The following month, one of our seminar attendees used our specialists in a case in Manchester against AIB involving fraud and won. Some months later, in Dublin, the exact same case was dropped by AIB. Over the coming months more of our clients realised how they too were being robbed by the banks, conned into buying properties by bank managers with undisclosed interests, overcharged by hundreds of thousands of euro and mis-sold financial products resulting in losses of millions of euro. With each client came more stories of corruption exposing the cosy relationship between the legal fraternity and the banks.

Soon after founding Legal & Equitable, we became involved in what has come to be regarded by many as the biggest case in banking history in Ireland: the Freeman case.

Sadly Miriam Freeman's unemployed status prevents her from being able to afford legal representation, unlike her bank who can boast of having the former attorney general of Ireland to represent them, not to mention having their expenses paid for by the Irish taxpayer whilst a woman is left to stand alone fighting for her home.

Then there are the two constitutional challenges, the first being against the Land and Conveyancing Law Reform Act 2013 (the Eviction Bill). Some of the arguments used in regard to this challenge is that it is retroactive, which means that the Irish Government want to backdate laws to facilitate the corrupt banking institutions. Furthermore, it denies the right to a plenary hearing or fair trial, which is contrary to the Constitution of Ireland and the European Courts of Human Rights and Justice.

We intend to bring a second challenge regarding the constitutionality of defendants forced to represent themselves against banks' counsel due to the unavailability of legal State aid, as identified by myself in over forty cases. These include mothers trying to fend off the banks attempting to make them and their children homeless. Penniless or on social welfare, the State nonetheless refuses them counsel, and yet pays top barristers and solicitors' firms millions of euro to represent the same banks that want to render our citizens homeless.

The following is a mantra I have recited to the annoyance of judges.

'Before I start, as with every case I attend, I would like to identify the inequality of my position. I stand here today unqualified as a solicitor, uneducated as a barrister, lacking in skills and knowledge and expertise in law, inferior because of my lack of understanding of the legal process, through desperation and fear of losing my family home, my life's work and my family. I will try to match the eminent Mr West, the wealth of people with superior knowledge and skill and the reputable firm that sit opposite me. I stand here today in a building where inequality is abhorred and punished, where the Constitution of this country is upheld guarantees the rights of all the persons in this State to be treated equally under Article 40 of the Constitution, which declares that all citizens in Ireland shall be held equal before the law. This means that the State cannot unjustly, unreasonably or arbitrarily discriminate between citizens nor can they be treated as inferior or superior to any other person in society because of their human attributes or ethnic, racial, social or religious backgrounds. I have sought redress from the President of the Law Society, the Attorney General, the President of the High Court without reply. I have sought redress from the President of Ireland whose office was established to protect the very Constitution I have just referred to, who pledged solemnly to uphold the Irish Constitution. I ask you, is what I am about to do today here reasonable, just or equal in light of such inequality that must be obvious to everyone before me, sitting at the bench? I ask you the question; is this just, fair or equal?

No response was ever given.

There is also the Bank of Scotland (Ireland) case regarding registration of title and the O'Donnell case that intends to go before the European Court of Human Rights. If adequately funded, Legal & Equitable will bring cases against registrars who acted as sheriffs, as well as against the agents of the sheriff who acted contrary to statute law. We also intend to hold a national conference in 2016 to inform the citizens of this nation of their rights.

4

Eviction, Twenty-first-Century Irish Style

It was to be expected that my Supreme Court win in 2013 would attract the attention of other homeowners who found themselves in a similar situation to what I had been in twelve months earlier. Since that November, I had been inundated with emails, texts and unannounced visits from frightened individuals. Mothers cried on my doorstep and men begged for help as my heart constricted at hearing yet another story of a family awaiting to be ejected from their homes and disposed of like refuse. Such was the frequency of these visits that by early 2014 I had become a sponge to stories of ruination – my own was now mirrored in the lives of the thousands of people who sought my advice.

Usually meeting in the local hotel, before speaking I could see how each couple's body language spoke of their pain. With embarrassment etched across the man's face, his partner would look away from him as her desire to protect their children from homelessness took precedence. With her tear-stained face camouflaged sparingly with make-up, the absence of wedding bands (sold or pawned) indicated just how desperate their situation had become. Before they uttered a word, I knew their story.

These are people, who, having been made redundant or forced to accept severe pay cuts, soon fall into arrears with their mortgage payments. Following the initial shock at being unable to pay their bills, panic sets in, then disbelief, which sometimes leads to depression. Smothered in self-loathing, underpinned by a sense of helplessness, the future looks daunting as the bank refuses to negotiate but, rather, continues to send threatening letters and abusive phone calls on a daily basis.

From that first demand letter, followed by a special summons by the banks' solicitors, the legal fraternity's cash register rings louder and louder, as their billable hours increase with each correspondence sent on their client's behalf, for which you, the borrower, will pay. Not unlike an army marching towards the enemy, each communication received indicates a move closer towards possession of your family home and the prospect of complete financial ruin. However, unlike the traditional armaments of battle, against which an opponent can mount a defence with some prospect of success, there can be no victory against the banks whose collaboration with the Government and legal system ensures that they almost always emerge victorious. For the weaponry of this new type of battle is psychological warfare supported by unlimited financial resources. From banks seeking possession orders to the appointment of receivers to take farms and businesses, the prospect of a visit from the sheriff is akin to waiting on death row to be executed for a crime you did not commit. At least on death row there is an entitlement to legal representation, unlike being pitted against the banks where the individual finds themselves wandering in a legal wasteland with nowhere to run and not knowing who to trust. For how else can it be when the average cost of a solicitor is €300 per hour?

So, when I receive over two hundred emails per week from people seeking free legal advice, I would like to believe it is because of my experiences within the courts, whereas it has more to do with the fact that basic legal representation is neither affordable nor accessible in Ireland.

If there was a date that signified the beginning of the end for homeowners in arrears with their mortgage, it was 25 July 2013; for on that day our Labour President, Michael D. Higgins. signed into law the legislation that has legalised eviction in Ireland and in doing so legitimised the carnage that followed in its wake. Contained within a six-page document, the reintroduction of eviction was on instruction from the Troika, who were looking for a way to recapitalise the banks, but first they had to reinstate the law required to grant possession of a property that had been removed by Ms Justice Elizabeth Dunne in 2011. It was this void in law, or lacuna that had thus far protected homeowners in arrears. (The Troika was a decision group formed by European Commission (EC), the European Central Bank (ECB) and the International Monetary Fund (IMF) whose purpose was to assess 'compliance' with the reforms and budget cuts required for each part of the Irish bailout.)

Hoping to create media attention, I brought an inter-locutory injunction against President Higgins's signing of this Bill and how his swearing of the same oath as the men and women who sacrificed their lives for our freedom was nothing short of political treason.

Here is what your President had to say:

Dear Mr Darcy,
Thank you for your email. I regret to have to inform you that by virtue of the doctrine of separation of powers of the State it is not open to the President to intervene in matters which are the responsibility of the Courts. I hope you will understand the position and am sorry that this Office cannot assist you further.
Yours sincerely,
Linda Farrell
Secretariat

To Ms Farrell,

The presidential oath of office is to uphold the Irish Constitution. Can you confirm that the President of Ireland cannot intervene, comment or contact his government on this travesty that befalls the men and women of this country? It is his obligation to do this for his citizens as well his legal, moral and social obligation.

I await your reply,

Tom Darcy

Dear Mr Darcy,

I refer to your email of 9th May 2012 to President Higgins concerning Articles 40 and 41 of the Constitution.

I regret to have to inform you that the President by virtue of his Constitutional position is precluded from intervening in matters which fall within the remit of the Courts. I hope you will understand the position.

Yours sincerely,

Linda Farrell

To the President of Ireland

A Chara,

In accordance with Article 40 of the Irish Constitution, I seek your immediate intervention into the perpetration by the courts of this state for ignoring my right as an Irish citizen under Constitution Article 40 to be treated equally and fairly. As a lay litigant, I do not hold the knowledge or expertise required to equally defend my family and myself, and it is illegal for me to hold myself as a barrister or solicitor, but yet I am compelled to do so for the sake of my family against the legal fraternity who are paid by your citizens.

There is no provision within the courts of Ireland for legal representation in a civil case for defendants who are without financial support. I have reported this to the president of the

Law Society and the Attorney General without reply. My family are entitled, under the Constitution, Article 41, to be recognised 'as the natural primary and fundamental unit group of society, and as a moral institution possessing inalienable and imprescriptible rights, antecedent and superior to all positive law'. My family and thousands of your citizens' families' constitutional rights are being violated daily resulting in their eviction, fragmentation and desecration. As your oath of office states, you are to uphold the Irish Constitution. I now ask you to do what you solemnly pledged. Failure to respond or act on this travesty and exploitation of your citizens' constitutional rights surmounts to ignoring your oath of office and the Irish Constitution.

You will note I attached a letter to your Minister for Finance Michael Noonan.

Tom Darcy

No response followed and together with a silent media the lacuna in law no longer protected family homes. Parents with nowhere to go now faced the indignity of packing their family's life into black sacks on the side of the road, while the sheriff hands their keys to the bank official, exchanges paperwork and proceeds to sell their home in a fire sale for a fraction of its value. The bank then claims all of the mortgage lent and legal costs as a tax loss (even though they sold it and were compensated for it by uninformed taxpayers) with the homeowner being held responsible for the full balance.

Within weeks of the legislation being passed my inbox was full. Such was the aggression of the Irish banks towards their customers that words like 'suicidal', 'fear' and 'guilt' peppered the messages, which were mainly from distressed couples or a parent suffering physically or mentally. All shared their stories with me like I was their best friend, whereas in truth I was possibly the only person whom they believed would be on their side against the banks. Helpless and isolated, what they needed was an outstretched hand offering hope. On average, two pages in length, whole lives would be condensed into paragraphs, often starting with children's names and ages. Once proud, working parents, they were now exhausted after months of tactical warfare against the banks' legal army. Regardless of the hundreds of homeowners I had come to befriend over the years, I never became immune to their stories of humiliation and poverty. Suffering with insomnia spawned from fear, their anxiety was carpeted by depression and their anger fuelled by the wasted months in defence against an aggressor who was well recompensed for their actions and empowered to continue. In full knowledge of the callousness of the legal fraternity, I would piece together their defence as though it were my own, and in the process I unearthed the truth behind the architects of the Irish property crash.

By 2009, as the property boom was beginning to wane, words and phrases like 'austerity' and 'pay cuts' were being bandied around. It was no surprise then that those who had bought during the boom would find themselves in financial trouble. As well as being unable to meet their monthly repayments, the banks themselves were, in the main, unwilling to negotiate. There are many stories of how banks hounded customers for money they did not have and yet refused to broker a mutually acceptable deal. The result of which was jingle mail, where people surrendered their keys and left the country while others began the long process of bankruptcy abroad, and then there were those who took on the banks and who subsequently became the target of the sheriff and his security men.

Initially ignored by the mainstream media, at first the number of mortgage defaulters was sufficiently low so as to be dismissed as a minority of investors who had 'over-stretched' themselves during the boom with their 'ambitious property portfolios'. However, it soon became apparent that those who had the most to lose in the housing market were buyers whose sole purchase had been their family home, and, unlike property investors who might lose their assets, whole families now faced eviction.

There is nothing more profoundly shocking to our sense of security than the prospect of losing our home, not just our house or apartment, but the place we live, share with others, raise our family and work to pay for. If this is under threat, then so too are all other aspects of our lives. Where will we live and where will our children live? How will we manage to go to work? Who will provide our next home? The implications of losing a home, then, are not simply confined to the possession of a property, as the banks would have us believe, but include the devastation of whole families who did nothing wrong.

These were people who had purchased in good faith under the advisement of a mortgage broker who was, more often than not, working on commission so that the more 'mortgage products' they sold, the more money they earned. With the result that they could neither claim impartiality nor furnishing advice in the best interest of their customers and what they could realistically afford; rather, in an effort to meet sales targets, all manner of 'potential income' would be created and taken into account in order to assure the maximum loan. As much of this income was seasonal, the new homeowner soon found themselves in trouble when their salary was cut or when they were laid off altogether, but that did not matter to the salesmen and women of our banking sector whose preoccupation with quarterly sales figures had managed to silence the voice of their conscience.

Due to the acceleration of mortgage defaults since the property crash, it would be expected that the media would assume its investigative role in exposing the banking corruption that had facilitated the lending of huge amounts of money. By highlighting the public's awareness of the societal damage should this problem be ignored, the banks would be compelled to negotiate with customers and allow them to remain in the family home and so prevent whole communities from collapsing into a downward spiral of homelessness, bankruptcy, family break-up, mental health issues and suicide. Although references were periodically made to the increasing number of mortgage arrears, while being discussed within a context of the 'housing crisis' and 'economic downturn', the true horror of what homeowners were experiencing could be neatly sidestepped; namely, the financial ruin of customers who trusted their banks and those who represented them.

It then appeared that it would be left to our recently launched television channel, UTV Ireland, to demonstrate impartiality towards real issues that would come under the scrutiny of its own journalists. One issue should have been the possession orders sought for one hundred and ten family homes in Castlebar Courthouse, Mayo, in March 2015. With honest and diligent reporting, we would hope to learn how the fate of whole families was sealed by the illegal penning of documents by county registrar Fintan Murphy, given that only a judge should sign eviction orders of a family home. We would also hope to learn how the same registrar then assumed the role of sheriff, which allowed him to execute his own orders, for which he was paid by the banks. That is right, Fintan Murphy gets paid per eviction order. Indeed, the position of sheriff originated under British Rule and was the chief executive officer of the British Crown. It could be said that ongoing evictions were repugnant to the beliefs of the

Irish Free State and had directly contributed to the Easter Rebellion. Disappointingly, however, the reporter chose not to focus on the devastation caused to our own people but rather on the 'disruptions in the Castlebar Courthouse', 'sympathetic banks' and 'compassionate registrar'.

At this point, it is important to remember that the Irish Courts, established under Article 34 of the Irish Constitution, is part of a tripartite separation of powers: the legislature, the executive and the judiciary. The Government is the organ of State exercising the executive power of government, the two houses of parliament comprising the Oireachtas (of which the President is the titular head, in addition to his or her constitutional status as head of state) exercise the legislative power of government, and the Courts established by Article 34 of the Constitution exercise the judicial power of government. This ensures that no one organ of State may interfere with the functions ascribed to the other two. So what happens when the judiciary exercise the Government's power that is subsequently used to enforce their own orders? Such would be the case if a registrar were to double job as a sheriff, like Mairéad Ahern, who, in her capacity as registrar for County Louth and County Meath grants possession of families' homes in the morning (for which she is paid by the taxpayer), and then in the afternoon executes the same orders as county sheriff (for which she is paid by the banks). So she signs the legal documentation to throw families out onto the streets in the morning and in the afternoon ensures that they are physically thrown onto the streets. Furthermore, it is Mairéad Ahern's husband's law firm, Ahern & McDonnell Solicitors, that brings the bulk of the possession orders into court. Presented in the morning, applications for possession are signed by his wife and in the afternoon are executed by her, for which he is paid by the banks.

At this juncture let us look at Mairéad Ahern's salary and the cost of her 'public service'. She is paid an annual average salary of €125,000 for her role as registrar in County Louth, and we can only assume that she earns the same amount for the same role in County Meath. Then there is her salary as a sheriff: in Ireland the sheriff's fee is based on 'poundage', which is 5 per cent for the first €5,500 and 2½ per cent for the remainder of the order of the court, which covers all the debt plus expenses such as staff and locksmiths, as laid down in the Sheriff's Fees and Expenses Order 2005. So, were a family to be evicted from a home with a mortgage of €400,000 plus legal fees and interest (another €100,000), the sheriff would receive 5 per cent of the first €5,500, which is €275, and 2½ per cent of the remaining €494,500, which is €12,362.50. Together this gives a total of €12,636.50. Given that it would not be unusual for the granting of up to ninety possession orders in one week and assuming that each would be based on the average mortgage, it follows that from one week's work alone, Mairéad Ahern could earn €1,137,375. Then there are the court orders for properties worth in excess of €400,000 and, taking into account the average working year of forty weeks, perhaps some journalist would like to investigate how many court orders were issued by Mairéad Ahern in 2014, from which could be calculated the exact amount paid into the Ahern household by the Irish taxpayer. By the evidence so far, there certainly appears to be a strong financial incentive for registrars/sheriffs to continue evicting families from their homes and thereby perpetuating the cycle of homelessness, mental illness, marriage and family break-up as well as suicides that follows in its wake.

In light of which, although it would be untrue to claim that the media is totally ignoring the social impact of banking corruption in Ireland, by skirting around the issue they can

avoid bringing those responsible to account for the return of
the stick that throughout the centuries had been used to beat
the Irish people; the same stick that kept us weak and
vulnerable unable to prosper economically and that excluded
us from the world stage of social, scientific and technological
progress. This is the stick of eviction.

The following paragraphs look at how the return of
eviction to Ireland has started the process of destabilising our
nation all over again. Only this time it is not the absentee
landlord who arrives with the local constabulary, but a
domestic enemy whose subversion has allowed them to go
unnoticed until now, until they began to wave the weapon of
our historical oppression in front of us.

It has taken a long time for the Irish people to turn to their
own people with pointed finger, but the evidence is
irrefutable. It stretches from the Land and Conveyancing Law
Reform Act 2013, which allows for eviction in Ireland, to the
criminal behaviour of an unregulated banking sector who lent
billions of euro to people who they knew could never pay it
back and to the solicitors, barristers and judges who are
themselves so deeply financially indebted to the banks that
their impartiality can no longer be assured. There is no doubt
that this system operates like little more than a national cartel.

'I rule, I'm not biased', stated a judge recently when asked
whether or not he himself was biased in favour of the banks.
It appears that only in Ireland could such a statement be made
in court and go unchallenged or unreported. Together with
their own property empires, millions of euro in banking shares
and their appointment to cases at the request of banks'
solicitors, we have sitting on the benches, Government
appointed judges who remain untouchable. In plain sight, the
names of judges and their spouses appear on building portfolios
in Land Registry offices in Ireland. In negative equity to the

tune of millions of euro, questions must be raised as to the possibility of sweetheart deals or the promise of write-downs or write-offs in lieu of unspoken favours. It is no surprise then to see a barrister's frown turn to a smile when they learn who has been appointed to hear their case.

What do these groups of politicians, bankers and judges expect to happen as a result of making whole families homeless and reducing tens of thousands more to financial ruin? What is the sense in making our country bankrupt – is there a plan? Or maybe it is just corruption on a monumental scale that has no particular end in sight, only the further lining of the pockets of those who sign eviction orders and then receive massive pensions after a few short years of service. Whatever the reason, it is time that we became aware of how the reintroduction of eviction in Ireland is weakening our society by spreading fear throughout whole communities. For as the tenant once dreaded the arrival of the landlord and his constables, thousands of homeowners now fear the arrival of the sheriff and his security men, leaving us wondering how much has changed in the last few generations in the balance of power between the governed and those who claim to govern us, the people.

Deeply embedded within the Irish psyche, the prospect of eviction instilled terror in the heart of our ancestors who from year to year eked out a meagre existence on the land. Regardless of the output, the rise in annual rents held the threat of eviction over whole communities, particularly with rack-renting, when rent would be deliberately raised beyond what the tenant could afford with the intention of eviction so that the land could be returned to pasture.

With nowhere to go, it was emigration or the workhouse, where children over three years of age were separated from their parents. Inmates, as they were referred to, worked an eleven-hour day and lived in damp, unsanitary conditions where whooping cough, influenza, typhus and dysentery were rife. However, such was the poverty in Ireland that regardless of the horrors within the walls of these places, by 1846 most workhouses were oversubscribed with thousands of people being turned away. By 1848, at the height of the Great Famine, there were approximately a quarter of a million Irish people in workhouses.

Although confined to the pages of history books, it is important to remember that within our country's long and established history these events are relatively recent. For it was only five generations ago, when during the Great Famine, that whole families starved to death or emigrated. For those who chose to stay on the land, their lives were made impossible by landlords who wanted the land back, and who sometimes offered to pay for their passage to America in order to get them off the land. Although there were some landlords who did come to the aid of their tenants, such was the national pain resulting from the forced movement of the Irish people that soon after the famine the Land League (1879) was formed, bringing the issue of security of tenure to the forefront of Irish politics.

According to its founder Michael Davitt (1846–1906), 'the land question can be definitely settled only by making the cultivators of the soil proprietors'. With that as the ultimate aim, the Three Fs (fair rent, fixity of tenure and free sale) became the purpose of the Land League of Mayo, which was founded with the support of Charles Stewart Parnell, leader of the Irish Parliamentary Party and also a chief campaigner for Home Rule. He was later to become president of the National Land League and by uniting all land agitators it was to become a formidable political force in Ireland. One of their most famous successes was the ostracising of land agent

Captain Charles Boycott, which resulted in him abandoning Ireland. Progress was also due to Davitt's relentless campaigns and fearless speeches, which regularly led to his arrest, imprisonment, release and rearrest, all of which drew greater attention to the land question, until finally in 1881 the Land Act granted the Three Fs.

In light of which, when we talk about eviction, we are not just discussing the impact upon particular families or even the decimation of whole communities, but how the inherent lack of security that is implied in being able to be removed from our homes and the land oppressed us as a nation economically, socially and culturally. For when the goal is to merely survive from day-to-day, there is little prospect of anything else, least of all the creation of entrepreneurial opportunities or cultural endeavours. It was only when we emigrated and freed ourselves from the constraints of our oppressor did we create anew. From careers in public service to national service or more entrepreneurial activities, Irish names grace the history books of adopted countries, indicating not only the great spirit of our people but how that spirit had been so suppressed in our native land.

So, when our history books show us an image of a family being evicted, we are looking at a snapshot of an entire nation that arguably took a long time to recover from generational oppression, and when we did finally begin to consider our place among the nations of Europe, the reality of eviction returned. Just as our head was inching above the parapet, our oppressor returned, though not in the form of English landlords entering and violating a family home, but in the form of our banking, legal and governmental institutions who, with the support of the local sheriff and his security men, continue to ruin family homes and publicly humiliate those within. Occasionally the owner-occupier is notified directly and is told to pack their stuff and get ready to be evicted by those who are non-responsive to pleas from mothers, but who smile wider as they force a father down on his knees to beg for mercy; such public emasculation is not uncommon during an eviction. For their amusement the sheriff and his security men frequently attempt to exert maximum humiliation on parents, often recording their pleas on their phone and then playing it back to them, laughing. These are the men who are now filling the shoes of history's collaborators, the twenty-first-century bogymen sent to terrify homeowners in order to spread fear throughout communities. Having found myself in this position, I can vouch for the paralysing fear that accompanies an attempted eviction, where an attack upon a peaceful neighbourhood is played out.

5

Stories of Eviction

As soon as the sheriff arrives, an SOS is sent to all social media sites.

'It's on, sheriff here, need help.'

We stand together, shoulder to shoulder, armed only with the laws of Ireland, demanding the paperwork that can rarely be produced and quoting the law of 1926, prohibiting security guards from trespassing on private property in the absence of official engagement. As reinforcements swell our numbers, the hunter begins to feel his vulnerability. Although the sheriff and his security men are usually forced into retreat, tomorrow holds the possibility of their return. Some of us will stay the night, sleeping on a couch or floor, offering peace of mind to the homeowner.

When a child is ejected from their primary sanctuary, life is lived with a foreboding that no matter how tightly we hold onto what we have, it can be taken from us. Such is the case for forty-six-year-old Robert. In 1975, Robert's father took ill and died leaving a young mother and four boys, of whom Robert was the eldest. He vividly recalls the white piece of paper and the name of the undertaker on the top, as well as his mother's tears as she held it each night, unable to pay the funeral costs. With no money to pay the electricity bill, candles had to suffice, as did branches and twigs from the park that replaced the turf in the fireplace. Coddle followed as a staple diet, and sometimes stewing meat and a half pound of potatoes and carrots were donated by relatives with patronising smiles. Then there were trips to the social welfare clinic begging for money, where Robert and his siblings sat in second-hand clothes that had arrived in hard brown paper.

'Once, Mammy and I went to the pawn shop,' Robert told me, 'and she cried as she handed over the rings that Daddy had given her. Christmas meant jigsaws and fruit or a bag of chocolates to be shared. Then there was the thunder-like sound on the frontdoor as giant men lifted us out of our beds, while we cried and stood outside barefoot in the cold in our pyjamas. Mrs Egan from next door held Mammy as she cried. When our sofa was dumped on its back, I saw the tears in it where Mammy's hand had rummaged for coins for the gas metre. For the next three years we lived in Mrs Egan's shed; Mickey, my baby brother and Adrian stayed in her house during the winter months. My teenage years were spent working on a milk float and then driving a bus. Matthew, my next brother, worked for twenty years and took his own life days after he was made redundant, such was his fear of being evicted again. My own disposition was inherited by my children, who panic when there is a knock on the door.'

SOS in Finglas on the Northside of Dublin – the address appears on Facebook with the alert, 'sheriff en route'. As the network of likeminded people are activated, transport is provided and we arrive into a situation where there is no information, only a last-minute appeal from a woman with four children. As neighbours identify the house in question, I see the sheriff's black Ford Focus parked alongside four white security vans whose occupants are creating a ring around the front of the house. Nearby are the men of Dyno-Locks, the commercial company hired by the sheriff to drill the locks off the doors, trying to look inconspicuous as they await instructions.

Experience has taught me the futility of engaging with collaborators, so with the neighbour's permission, I go through her house and jump over the garden wall. With a two-metre fence to climb, I grab each side and use it as a makeshift ladder, then jump over the fence and into the back garden. Peering in the back window, I see young children huddled under the kitchen table with half-emptied breakfast bowls. Identifying myself, the lady, still in her nightclothes, opens the back door. Wrapping her arms around me, she cries, 'I didn't know what to do.' Trying to console her, I need as much information about the situation as possible; for through the front window the backs of the collaborators are seen inching their way towards us, at which point the sheriff knocks on the door. Placing a table behind me to prevent a storming of the house, I greet him.

'Good morning,' I say, with my hand on the lock to prevent drilling, 'can you show me your identification please?'

The sheriff shakes his head as his security men try to push their way in.

'This man will not show me any identification,' I shout to the crowd, using my request as a delaying tactic while waiting for reinforcements to arrive. Hearing the woman behind me pleading with the men not to hurt her children, our own men take my route so that by the time I ask to see the paperwork we stand six and growing. Displaying a possession order in her husband's name, I again raise my voice to the crowd:

'This is not valid,' I say. 'This order is naming the husband who doesn't live here any more.'

The sheriff is thwarted by his own error, and by now the crowd has swelled in numbers behind him. We're in the heart of a former well-known IRA community and I know just what to say next.

'This man is using a British order to try and evict this innocent Irish woman.'

Incensed, the crowd pushes through the wall of security men as the Gardaí call for back-up. The sheriff breaks into a run, but the force of the crowd sways his car backwards and forwards before allowing him to go. He does not return.

A few weeks later I had just left a house in Tallaght, Dublin that was owned by a young couple. Recently unemployed, their family home had become a war zone of blame. For it is inevitable, when trapped in such a position we argue with those closest to us. Sitting in the car, I glanced back at the mother holding her baby's hand and waving me goodbye. A moment of nostalgia of when my own sons were babies was interrupted by my mobile phone ringing.

'Tom, can you get to Swords? Sheriff evicting elderly couple.'

Upon my arrival, four of our team were already present. I approached the security man standing at the door.

'You, no go,' I was told, but upon taking out my phone to record him, he retreated. Walking past the sheriff, I introduced myself to the couple. Silver-haired and eloquent, they sat together holding hands. They were a former teacher and civil servant, who five years previously had acted as guarantor for their son's house, but, having recently lost his job, he had emmigrated to New Zealand leaving a tenant installed along with a verbal agreement with the bank for interest-only payments. However, the bank then decided to call in the full mortgage and weeks later the son's house was sold in a fire sale for a fifth of the original value: €80,000 and now they were coming after his parents for the balance on foot of the guarantee.

Letters were piled high on the side table. Unable to legally defend themselves, they had left the letters unopened. Apparently, their son had borrowed €400,000 and had arrears of €96,000. The bank now wanted €416,000 plus costs. The value of the couple's house was estimated at €300,000, the loss of which would leave them homeless as well as owing a residual debt of over €116,000 plus costs. I sat with the couple, whose embarrassment could be felt by all present. With their frail hands shaking, the husband asked me how bad it was. Not answering immediately, I walked to the front door to see how the others were getting on. Peering down the side of the house, I noticed that their kitchen extension was overhanging their neighbour's perimeter wall. Enquiring as to whether or not they were on good terms with their neighbour, the couple confirmed that they were the best of friends. So I took out my laptop and drafted a plenary summons and a statement of claim for the neighbour, knowing that it would allow *lis pendens*, which is a tag placed on the property in the Land Registry identifying that litigation has been initiated. And since a house with a bad title cannot be sold, it would be of no use to the bank. An interlocutory injunction was also placed against the sheriff, who, by 5 p.m., had retreated. Sadly, two months later, the elderly husband passed away, but such was the strength of the statement of claim from the neighbour that the bank was forced into negotiation with the wife, who now lives in a granny flat at the side of her daughter's home.

Late one Thursday evening in August 2013 a private number appeared on my phone. Tempted to let it go to voicemail, I nonetheless pressed accept.

'Tom, I'm Luke Dwyer, the sheriff just left a voicemail saying he has taken my home, changed the locks and for me to collect my belongings. He rang from my home number.' According to Luke's neighbour, soon after leaving for work that morning, en route to which Luke had dropped off his wife and children at her mother's for breakfast, the sheriff had arrived with his security men. Drilling the front door lock, they had begun the process of loading everything out. Enquiring as to what they were doing, a neighbour was told that they were 'fucking out a scrounger'. Unwilling to get involved, she nonetheless recorded events on her camera phone.

Apparently the bank had been accepting interest-only payments on Luke's mortgage but then demanded the full amount of €2,300 per month. Initially, with his wife working full-time, this amount had not overstretched them but having lost her job in late 2009 and being unable to secure work since, the situation had continued to deteriorate. Not wanting to cause anxiety, Luke had been hiding the letters, as well as his own head in the sand. The availability of free legal advice would no doubt have encouraged him to deal with the issue, but having no one to turn to Luke even considered taking his own life, believing that his family might get some compensation. Little did he know that the bank would take anything his family would receive on his passing before they could access it.

After contacting other anti-eviction group members, I told Luke to keep his family away for the next twenty-four hours. Taking back his house would not be easy but would require a mandatory knowledge of the law and a lot of muscle flexing. Upon my arrival, I saw Luke's family life on display for all to see. Sofas, bags, a television, cots, buggies, beds, a washing machine and the contents of the kitchen cupboards and bedroom drawers were all piled in a heap in the front garden.

Our plan was to access the house through the back door and then open the front door from inside. Alan had been the first from our group to arrive at the scene. Luke and I arrived soon after, followed by six more from Louth. As Alan and I were directed down the back lane of Luke's house, the others walked up to the front door. Banging loudly on the window, Jimmy roared at the security guards inside.

'What did you do to my stuff? Get out or I'll fuckin' kill ye.' Terrified, they left. A master locksmith, Alan had the back door open in under thirty seconds, exposing a home that in a matter of hours had been completely cleared.

As we moved the last piece of furniture back into the house, the sheriff and his convoy of security vans arrived with the Gardaí close behind. On cue, the sheriff presented the eviction notice to the Gardaí only to be interrupted by our Jimmy from Louth, whose strong accent made every word sound increasingly menacing.

'Are ye the fucker who fucked out my stuff?'

The sheriff asked who they were.

'I'm Luke's tenant and you have no order for me.'

At which point, the Gardaí took their usual stance that it was a civil matter and backed away with Luke calling after them.

'Are ye not going to arrest these fuckers for breaking and entering?' Turning to the sheriff, Jimmy smiled.

'I'm a tenant in this house, and I'm inviting Luke and his wife back in.' He then slammed the door.

On the grass verge outside, raised voices could be heard between the sheriff and the Gardaí, only to be interrupted by Luke's new tenant opening the door and roaring at them. 'Get the fuck away from the front garden, this is private property.' Weary, by 8 p.m. the sheriff had left. Three of the anti-eviction team remained in the house during the following two weeks, which gave me time to write up the wife's motion for an injunction to form a case. The last time we spoke Luke's marriage had broken down, as his wife could not live with the fear of another sheriff's visit and the public humiliation. They had both returned to their respective parents' homes and put their house up for sale.

What about An Garda Síochána? Is it possible that they too have a role to play in reinforcing the connection between the banks, the Government and the legal fraternity? Whether it is standing by while families are thrown onto the street or assisting with unlawful arrests and detentions, it seems that the Gardaí are equally complicit in the ruination of whole families and individuals like Andrew Delahunt. He had already been illegally incarcerated for nearly a month when I received a phone call from Jerry Beades asking me to support his friend who was up in front of Judge Gilligan the following day.

Arriving early, Jerry filled me in on the details. Apparently, one Monday morning, the Gardaí had arrived in convoy to arrest Andrew on his farm. Handcuffed in front of his children and bundled into the back of a police van, he was taken to Mountjoy Prison where he was accused of being in contempt of a court order he knew nothing about. Prior to this, the banks had been threatening Andrew for months. Owing €230,000 on his mortgage, and despite his pleas for reduced payments, the bank was already eyeing up his prime land.

As soon as the receiver, George White, had been appointed (a position which he was neither qualified nor experienced), he sought an injunction against Andrew in order to prevent him 'interfering with him and his security men'. Being an ex-parte application, it meant that Andrew was unaware of its existence. On receipt of which (with no evidence required by the judge), George White arrived at Andrew's farm accompanied by four vehicles in military convoy. Surrounded by security men, he handed Andrew proof of his own appointment as receiver and then proceeded to walk around taking an inventory while ignoring Andrew's questions. That same afternoon, George White went to the Garda Station and made a complaint that Andrew had interfered with him doing his job, which was contrary to the court order. The Gardaí arrived the following morning to arrest Andrew for breaching the order he did not know about.

Escorted either side by prison guards, incoherent and clearly traumatised, Andrew stood in the same clothes he had worn to prison twenty-six days earlier. Jerry and I sought to have Andrew's imprisonment quashed given that he had been arrested without a warrant. That is right: Andrew had spent almost a month in prison without any paperwork. Quoting the Irish Constitution that states that a person cannot be held in prison without an arrest warrant, Jerry asked how Andrew could have been in breach of an order he knew nothing about as well as being denied legal representation. In response, the barrister representing George White (compliments of the taxpayer) argued that the Gardaí only needed to be aware that such a warrant existed but did not need to have seen it or to present it. In other words, it need only exist in the mind of the Gardaí rather than in reality. Mr Justice Gilligan agreed with the requirement for only a mental image of a warrant and refused Andrew's application, returning him to the cells.

Remaining in the courtroom, I watched a total of six men that day who were standing in front of Judge Gilligan and being chastised for 'wasting the court's time' because they 'got the money and the banks have given them every chance to repay the loan and they must now vacate their homes and get on with their lives or face jail'. Knowing two of the men personally and how they had already staved off the sheriff prior to their arrest, I wondered if this was the latest tactic – to remove men from the family home, which left their wife and children vulnerable to the sheriff's next visit.

By early April Jerry and I were back in court. We desperately needed to get Andrew home as he was not coping well and was unable to get legal representation. As Andrew rested the weight of the metal handcuffs on the wooden table, Judge Gilligan slowly read the receiver's statement. The entire courtroom knew the truth of the situation, but apparently truth had no place in this room. Seeing as legal counsel had been denied him, Jerry Beades had been acting as Andrew's advocate, unlike the receiver who had in his corner the best legal team the Irish taxpayer could buy.

In his defence, Jerry again stated that Andrew knew nothing of an order obtained in his absence and that the Gardaí had removed him from his home without a warrant. After pausing, Judge Gilligan turned to Andrew and asked him whether he was willing to purge his contempt.

'You want me to lie?' Andrew asked. 'Okay, I will lie.' At which point he was handed the Holy Bible, and holding it between his hands he said: 'I swear I am lying when I say I did not know of the order and I further swear I will not interfere with the receiver.'

'You are free to go,' Judge Gilligan said, 'and remember you can be returned to prison if you interfere with the receiver.'

How ironic that most people end up in prison because they lie, but in the Irish courtroom a man has to lie to get out of prison. At the removal of his handcuffs, Andrew slowly wrapped his arms around his wife Kate. Outside the courtroom no victory was celebrated. Andrew just wanted to return to his family.

The consequences of Andrew's absence was clear when he arrived at his farm. With the lambing season having already begun, six lambs had been lost while he was in prison. The preparation the land had been missed, and there were weeks of hard toil ahead to get everything back in order. When Jerry and I finally left, Andrew's youngest daughter was holding onto his trouser leg with his wife close by. Unfortunately, this is not the end of the story of Andrew and his illegal imprisonment; the initial joy of his freedom was soon followed by the return of the receiver, who, this time, was going to ensure that no one stood in his way.

Three nights later an SOS from a sympathiser inside the receiver's office spread like wildfire through our network. Apparently an army of ex-military from several Eastern European countries had been assembled by the receiver to take Andrew's farm. Never before in this land of ours had such an action been mounted against a farmer and his family, nor did a community stand together as strongly as they did in the early hours of that morning to protect one of their own. The enemy may have been on their way, but an opposition was being mounted that would put pride back in the Irish heart.

Due to the guarantee given by Andrew that he would not interfere with the receiver's 'job', he reluctantly left his farm with his wife taking his place. By 1 a.m., behind the line of tractors and combine harvesters, a dozen men stood waiting. Nervous laughter filled the air while Kate and her neighbour provided tea and sandwiches, thanking each man who had given up his bed that night.

At 1.55 a.m. the sound of loud engines and barking dogs could be heard up the quiet country road. As each jeep and SUV parked in a line in front of the farm, over fifty men in balaclavas alighted. Standing in front of their jeeps and vans, each held onto a short leash with a snarling Alsatian at the end, only yards away from a dozen farmers.

From the windows of the farmhouse Kate watched this garrison of former warmongers. Crouched behind, her little children peered round the curtains at the glaring headlights and torches flickering over the heads of wild dogs waiting to attack. Contact with Andrew was via mobile phone; he was powerless to protect his family.

The receiver's pasty face soon appeared round the corner of the first combine harvester, shouting for the barriers to be removed, at which point blue flashing lights appeared from behind the squadron. An Garda Síochána had arrived, and a collective sigh of relief filled the night air. Our keepers of the peace and protectors of our laws made their way to the front. Although dwarfed in size and number by the foreign infantry, the presence of An Garda Síochána nonetheless released the tension of the night as a quick resolution was expected. And each man looked forward to returning to his family, who in his absence feared for his safety. But with the Gardaí speaking in hushed tones with the receiver and with their backs to the people, any assumption of protection was short-lived. Clearly, and without apology, each member of our police force stood beside the thugs from foreign lands. In that moment a feeling of collective shame filled the hearts of the men and women who stood against their oppressor. With their blue State uniforms, on which could be seen the badge of the Irish nation, they showed that the Constitution of Ireland, which had been fought for in blood and lost lives, counted for nothing.

The sheriff and his thugs were acting outside the law and supported by the courts, whilst the media remained silent. What else could be expected in light of the recent write-offs of millions of euro to Irish newspapers.

As the jeeps and SUVs departed at sunrise, members of An Garda Síochána informed Kate that her husband would be arrested on sight and she too could be imprisoned, at which point the farm would be seized. It appears that Andrew and his family were merely collateral damage in this financial cleansing. With this policy of internment becoming an integral fabric of the Irish judicial system, it seems that innocent parents can now be jailed at the behest of banks.

At 10 a.m., soon after the receiver and his thugs had left, Andrew walked into the Criminal Courts on Conyngham Road in Dublin. Although not yet convened, a judge had signed an arrest order during the night to ensure Andrew's immediate return to prison. At the same time, Mattie McGrath, an Independent TD who had fought for as many years as I against such injustice, had sent emails to the registrar and Minister for Justice overnight. The result was the dismissal of the court order. Aware that the previous night's activities could not be so easily covered up, the registrar of the court sent Andrew home to his family. Even so, Andrew will never be free from a criminal record, being in contempt of a court order he knew nothing about. Furthermore, in order to be released, he was forced to lie on the Bible.

The true nature of evictions twenty-first-century Irish style was never made clearer to me than the day I arrived at a stud farm in late 2013. An SOS had been received the previous evening on Facebook.

'Old age pensioner being evicted in the morning', it read, with no further details.

Living a few kilometres outside Leitrim town, Mary and John Doherty had borrowed €300,000 to build a house for their daughter and her children on their land. The broker who had sold the loan had been unregulated, as was the loan and the terms and conditions associated with it – for example, the clause that referred to the penalties of compound interest and administration fees that accrued should even one payment be missed. With the result that, less than a year later, after several missed payments (not to mention the billable hours it took to write letters from the bank's solicitors), the family now owed over €1.4 million.

An unregulated loan sold by an unregulated broker is not uncommon in Ireland, given that there are no official regulations within the banking sector and even the banking codes of practice need only be accepted voluntarily. Not unlike a murderer being offered a list of conditions for his approval should he wish to proceed with the crime, the banking sector can accept or reject regulations prior to all financial dealings. Then there are the laws that are regularly discarded for the sake of expediency, like the Family Home Protection Act 1976, which made it mandatory for each partner to receive independent advice so that the wife could not be placed under duress by her husband in regard to the family home. Fast forward three decades, when between 2005 and 2009 over 300,000 people got married. Eager to get on the property ladder, and given that some salaries had not caught up with prices, it was not uncommon for either set of parents to act as guarantor. However, instead of receiving independent advice, often the same solicitor worked for both parents together as well as their children and in many cases the bank and the developer as well. In some solicitors' offices, the first-time buyers could get a mortgage, a life insurance policy and legal advice on the same day. Furthermore, properties and land belonging to developers were often held back from registration as solicitors assumed they would be re-registered when sold on, thereby allowing them to pocket millions of euro in unpaid stamp duty and land registration fees.

Given such professional negligence, it is no wonder that we do not trust our legal system. With conveyancing having taken over from the slip-and-fall litigation business of ambulance-chasing solicitors, we now had the supply and demand of properties cornered and controlled by the banks – it was the perfect financial storm. Indeed, when speaking to mortgage holders, I ask them whether their solicitor is insured or if the contract has been changed or altered in any way. I ask each husband whether or not his wife received independent advice from another solicitor and if she understood the contract. And, finally, I enquire if they are aware that their lender is insolvent, unregulated, unlicensed, fraudulently returning accounts, misrepresenting their share value and not adhering to Irish banking regulations and statutory law.

With 100 per cent mortgages rolled out as quick as the ink could dry, due procedures and the law were often abandoned. After all, there was no time to waste offering independent advice when there were five hundred to six hundred mortgages to process per week, resulting in over half a million mortgages in a few short years. So with the paperwork of trainee solicitors going unchecked by trainee bankers, mistakes were inevitable. Contracts went unwitnessed, dates were omitted, and stamps failed to be endorsed leading to tens of thousands of people being overcharged. So rampant was this overcharging that An Garda Síochána was brought in to investigate the thousands of letters received by customers from banks admitting to overcharging interest. From just two hundred cases investigated, each customer had been overcharged from €30,000 to €1.4 million but no prosecutions followed. Therefore, when Mary's daughter fell into arrears, given that neither due procedure nor the law had been followed, the bank's case against them should have been dismissed. Instead of which, the bank was awarded a judgement against the home and farm.

I was unaware of the history on approaching Mary's farm that summer morning. Standing majestically against the backdrop of the Leitrim countryside, paddocks, white wooden fences and roaming hills concealed it well from passers-by. It was the place where Mary had lived with John their entire married life of forty-six years, and also where she had discovered his body a year earlier hanging from a tree in their garden. Such was his distress at the relentless letters and daily phone calls from the bank that he finally buckled under pressure, and such was Mary's grief that she lay under him for almost a whole day willing God to take her too. Around the home they shared could be found hundreds of letters from their bank, one of which was addressed to Mary's daughter, alleging that her mother had deceived her about the loan. The result of which is that Mary's daughter no longer speaks to her nor has Mary seen her grandchildren for over five years.

Part of an overall strategy, it is not uncommon for financial institutions to employ psychologists to create a web of mistrust between family members in order to scupper further attempts by them to protect their property. They can be found sitting inconspicuously at the back of courtrooms jotting down their observations; the litigant continues with their case as their emotional health and mental determination is assessed with frightening accuracy. According to one whistleblower, it is now a given that lay litigants can only take six court visits before 'cracking up'.

Psychologists also assess each family situation independently and how the trauma of a potential suicide could be used in their client's (the bank's) favour. They further gauge how this trauma can be manipulated in order to weaken the remaining family, leaving them defenceless against the sheriff and his security men whose wages and overtime are added to the mounting debt of the homeowner. The outcome of these courtroom observations are detailed reports to the banks outlining the most effective strategies that will result in the desired ends: namely a father too paralysed with fear to defend his home in the courts and too ashamed to have his life displayed on the road in front of neighbours. Once this level of paralysis is achieved, the legal dogs of war are free to savage any resistance that might remain, leaving the taxpayer to clean up the carcass of devastated families.

Unable to afford the standard hourly rate of €300–€400 for legal advice, and with a waiting list of one to two years by the voluntary groups, when faced with a possession application by the bank, the homeowner has only weeks to prepare their case. Regardless of Article 40 in our Constitution, which states that all citizens of Ireland must be treated equally, fairly and justly before the law, there is little doubt that the pending tsunami of unarmed victims are facing legal annihilation in the absence of publicly funded representation.

With parents trawling the Law Library in Dublin until closing time, grandparents must become surrogate parents to their grandchildren so that their own children can study and chat on legal forums in order to take on some of the most eminent solicitors and seasoned barristers in the country. Subsidised by the endless pockets of the banks, this is the same money that is gained through the sale of possessed houses. In other words, the banks are fighting the Irish people *with their own money.*

From my own observations, watching the banks' henchmen demolish a lay litigant is akin to watching a prize fighter get into the ring with a disabled man. Where is the honour in that? When the scales of justice are so unbalanced, how can victory be celebrated or justice done? But maybe neither justice nor victory are the objectives, but, rather, the annihilation of any opposition to the cabal that rules Ireland from behind the scenes, and which has turned the due legal process into a type of blood sport.

It sadly appears that the integrity of justice is abandoned once a lay litigant crosses the boundary of the Four Courts of Ireland, a place considered to be the national embodiment of a newly born republic. However, operating more like a marionette of a government that has deserted its people and constitution, it is a place where integrity can be purchased, impartiality compromised and compassion feigned by judges who follow not the law but direction by those too big to fail. With the cost of lodging an appeal having increased by 100

per cent in the past year, including €20 for an affidavit and
€10 more for your signature that has already been witnessed
many times, for the unemployed homeowner it is often a
choice between food and an appeal. Upon choosing the latter
you can then expect to be publicly humiliated in front of the
bank's legal team for not adhering to the court's orders to
produce alien documents whose cost could consume your
weekly sustenance. Indeed, the Troika themselves expressed
concern over the fees of the Irish legal fraternity, referring to
them as the highest paid in the world.

It was not until March 2015 that I learned about the billing
practices of some of our legal firms from one of their own. She
phoned me the morning after the airing of *Prime Time* on RTÉ
1, during which the president of the Bar Council rebuffed the
claim of exorbitant legal fees.

'Last night's interview was a pack of lies,' the woman at the
end of the phone began.

Claiming to work for one of the largest legal firms in Dublin,
she confirmed this by giving the senior partner's surname,
middle name and three phone lines to his office. Satisfied that
my new source was authentic, I listened attentively.

'My mentor is on €635 an hour. A five-minute phone call
to a client and he bills for an hour. Senior counsel can charge
anything from €1500 to €2000 per hour, even though most
of the work is just cut and paste. We bill a client up to €5000
for one meeting with counsel and two solicitors – one being
a junior who, although receiving €60 a day, our firm bills
€425 a day.'

She told me how clients are expected to give €25,000 up
front and by the time they reach court they would have paid
up to €100,000 in fees or costs.

Let us say that our client, Jane, wins in court and is awarded
costs. This means that her legal team's fees will be paid by the

court and they will, in turn, reimburse Jane the money she paid prior to her win. But, according to my new source, it is unlikely that Jane would receive back the full amount.

Assuming that Jane paid her legal team €100,000 before the case was heard, upon receiving costs the firm submits their costs to the taxing master at €150,000 knowing that it will probably be reduced), which it is by 20 per cent, leaving €120,000, which is €20,000 in excess of original costs (paid for by the client).

Jane is then informed that the fee was reduced by 20 per cent, which leads her to believe that it had been cut to €80,000. My whistleblower went on to say that the client is then told that the solicitor's fees cannot be paid out of the costs that are granted; they are more like personal fees that must be paid directly to the solicitor. Say that is another €20,000 which is taken directly out of costs. At the end of all that, the client is lucky to take home half of the fees they originally paid to the solicitor leaving some firms pocketing 150 per cent in fees.

I asked my whistleblower why she was telling me this.

'I'm giving up this job,' she said. 'I cannot stand the lies and deceit that is just accepted as normal. I have even heard opposition barristers planning how cases would turn out or how to extend a couple of more days in the courts in order to gain an extra couple of thousand. There is no justice, only greed.'

This is the reality for those who seek justice with no recourse to legal aid. For what type of defence allows a child to walk into a fire in full gaze of those who know her path?; wilful neglect, criminal negligence, contributory man-slaughter, terms quickly assigned to such barbaric behaviour, yet what else can be assumed of those who sit in judgement of lay litigants who are such children with limited legal knowledge?

I have witnessed many of these courtroom proceedings. I have seen grown men sobbing with hands clasped in front of judges as they set in motion the process that will break up their family, or individuals who know that they will never be free of the banks unless they leave their country never to return, effectively becoming exiles. This new blood sport can be witnessed in courtrooms all over Ireland on a daily basis, where intermittent nods between both legal teams followed by drinks in the local hotel indicate that they are in fact on the same side and are in court for the same reason: to ensure the possession of the family home of the person who has committed no crime nor broken any law. One wonders how a degree in law can be used as a weapon of national destruction, creating dishonourable courts with heartless judges who taunt defendants with Latin words and exclude them with legal language. No thought is given to the tens of thousands of Irish people who lie awake every night anticipating their turn in the legal arena.

It was into this same arena that Mary, at the age of sixty-four, would be thrust and where she would eventually become a formidable opponent, though not before facing down the sheriff and his security men.

At 8 a.m. we arrived at her farm in Leitrim. Where an entrance once existed, a Hadrian's Wall of hay now formed an impasse. Using camouflaging barrels of concrete, it included a secret entry point that led into a maze of hay corridors through which I and the other anti-eviction members navigated by phone. Continuing on to what seemed like dead ends, eventually sunlight was revealed. Here Mary met us with open arms. Emerging, I wondered if this was the Ireland that the diaspora longed to return to, where widows barricade themselves into their homes and not one public representative shout 'Stop'.

'Tom, I never expected you here,' she said as we embraced warmly. 'I have a big pot of tea for everyone inside.'

In spite of the reason for our visit, we could not help but be beguiled by Mary's farm and the house that stood majestically in the heart of the land which had been nurtured by the love that had filtered down through the generations. Momentarily transported to the Ireland of my youth, images of thatched roofs, whitewashed walls, half-doors and open turf fires filled my mind; they were comforting memories of families sharing what little they had and being happy together.

The house was complete with a bright-red door that opened to reveal a deceptively small country kitchen dominated by a pot-bellied stove and a large oak table in the middle of the room. The aroma of freshly baked bread and scones wafted through the air. We felt like young boys sitting at granny's table being fed treats before going outside to play make-believe war games. And, like our very own army general, Mary opened out her map of the farm and stretched it half way across the table, pointing to where our best vantage point would be in anticipation of the oncoming attack. I could not but smile at her tactical moves. Taking our places early, by 10 a.m. the first vehicle had entered the three hundred-yard driveway leading up to the farmhouse. Alerting each other on our mobiles, Mary disappeared and then reappeared on her tractor, driving at the oncoming van. Scrambling down the hayloft, our two hundred-yard dash to Mary was done at breakneck speed, and by which time she was already standing on her tractor telling the sheriff to get off her land.

Given the intimidating stance of Mary on her tractor, the sheriff obviously felt the need for more back-up. Within minutes three more vanloads arrived – they must have been sitting round the corner with their engines running. Again

Mary told them to get off her land, at which point over thirty men wearing balaclavas and carrying various types of weapons began to encircle the tractor as the Gardaí watched on. Jumping out of the hay fortress, I asked the sheriff for his name, identification and all documentation. It turned out that the signature at the end of the possession order was his own, which meant that he had signed his own order and was now trying to execute it in an attempt to bypass Mary's right to a fair trial. There he was: the judge, jury and executioner acting for the bank while being paid by the State and using the State's police force to protect his illegal actions. Referring to his security men, I asked the sheriff who they were. I was told that they were assisting him, which opened up the argument that he needed ministerial appointment to have such assistance as they were now trespassing. At this point, the Gardaí retreated to their patrol car and even more security vans arrived, turning the driveway into a carpark and in doing so rendered it impossible to access should an ambulance or other emergency service be required. Eight of us stood in a line for two hours until the Gardaí pulled the sheriff aside and spoke in hushed words. Slowly the collaborators returned to their vans but not before facing Mary and making the gesture of shooting a gun at her.

'That was a great morning's work, lads,' said Mary, clapping her hands, 'let's have lunch.'

We remained on the farm for the rest of the day, helping out with chores and enjoying the chance to spend time in the countryside. Paddy, one of our team, remained behind. Should the sheriff appear again, we estimated that Hadrian's Wall of hay would give us two hours to return and take up our places again. That night, however, petrol was poured on the hay and set alight. I was saddened, though not surprised. I had heard many such stories of farmers standing their ground against eviction only to suffer violence and intimidation until they surrendered their property 'voluntarily'.

It was the events the following Sunday, however that brought this intimidation to a new level. Arriving home from mass and her weekly visit to her husband's grave, Mary was greeted with a river of blood flowing down her driveway and onto the boreen outside. Falling to her knees, she could not bear to enter her property out of fear of what she would discover. Paddy, who had arrived down the previous evening, went in ahead of her. 'It's a bloodbath, Tom,' he said on the phone, his voice shaking. They decapitated her horses and the heads are strewn all over the farm. 'The fowl are dead too.'

I froze, visualising Mary covered in the blood of her pets, as she called them, which had been reared by herself and John. By the time the assailants were finished there was not one live animal left on her farm, nor was it fit for grazing because Mary's tractor had been used to track up the meadow, making it impossible for animals to walk with sure footing on the land. No arrests have been made to date as no witnesses came forward. Mary continues to fight the banks and has recently secured a solicitor and barrister to work *pro bono*. We wish her the very best.

6

Here's to My Whistleblowers

Despite the fact that the criminal activities of the banks and their puppet judiciary were on full display in our courts, it was the whistleblowers who held the key to exposing the relationship between them. During 2013 and 2014 I met several people who, for various reasons, wanted to share information with me. Citing the 'delicacy of the situation', they would go on to discuss the corruption they were witnessing at the highest level of our banking institutions. Offering 'sensitive information' for which they could 'easily lose their jobs', I would read how they 'didn't mean it to happen' and that they were 'only doing what they were told'. What they did not mean to happen was the financial ruin and perhaps suicide of former customers, which had resulted from the purchase of one or more of their financial products. Maybe it was this that had compelled them to offer substantial proof of financial corruption in exchange for the prospect of a full night's sleep.

Then there were whistleblowers who, being aware of my support towards homeowners in distress, simply wanted to remind me who was in charge. Without remorse they boasted about how the process of securitising a mortgage could 'yield a greater return than cocaine'. What my whistleblowers were referring to was the merry-go-round of money that was providing their spiralling commissions and uncapped bonuses, even though, as recently as 2013, South African Judge Selby Baqwa recommended that the practice of securitisation be criminalised in light of the role it played in the global economic crash. It is interesting to note that his common law jurisdiction is the same as in all common law countries, including Ireland, but no judge here appears to be willing to follow suit.

The best way to understand securitisation is to think of our friend, let's call him Bus Driver Bob, who, having fallen upon hard times, decides to pawn his gold watch to Charlie for €100 plus monthly interest payments. Charlie then takes out insurance (default insurance or indemnity insurance) which is paid out of the monthly interest, in case Bob cannot pay his monthly instalments. In order to make more money, Charlie then sells Bob's loan on to Mark (securitisation), who pays Charlie the €100 plus 33⅓ per cent, and with that €133 Charlie lends to another person and does the same thing again, meaning that he takes out insurance, sells on the loan, makes more money and with that money keeps lending. With every three loans, Charlie makes 100 per cent profit and still continues to receive interest payments each month from Bob and all the people to whom he lent, thereby creating money out of thin air. Charlie also manipulates interest rates resulting in overcharging and this causes Bob and everyone else to lose their jobs – leaving them unable to make their monthly interest payments. This means that Charlie can claim the default insurance on the loans he does not own any more because he sold them on to Mark (insurance fraud). Furthermore, Charlie claims a bailout and receives another 100 per cent of a loss he has not suffered. He then sues Bob and everyone else for breaching the loan agreement he no longer owns. Finally, Charlie sells on the list of people who took loans from him to a vulture company for a fraction of its value, say 30 cent on the euro.

A vulture company is a company with whom the original customer has no contract or agreement: such as Ulster Bank who acts as an agent for Tanager Limited, a vulture company which could comprise of retired credit managers. Now living on massive pensions (compliments of the taxpayer), they pick the bones of the same companies they forced into liquidation by buying their loans from the banks for cents in the euro; and then upon the companies falling into arrears, they pursue them for full repayment. Perhaps this could explain the reason why banks are unable to negotiate with customers any more. Is it because they no longer own the loan? It is only when a mortgage holder defaults that the question of ownership of the loan becomes an issue.

This is what happened to Colm, a thirty-four-year-old father of three working as a chef, who borrowed €300,000 from Bank of Scotland Ireland (BoSI) in mid-2008. Having gone into arrears, he soon heard from Tanager Limited, seeking the €300,000 plus €79,000 in arrears, all to be paid within ten days or face legal proceedings. Then there was Julie, a divorced mother of three in her thirties working as a waitress who had agreed to pay Tanager/BoSI Limited €30,000 euro over six years, but the following year they came after her for €150,000. David was another customer, a sixty-eight-year-old man; he openly disclosed that he suffered with Parkinson's disease and would be unable to return to work, but BoSI still approved a loan for €300,000.

However, what Tanager Limited had failed to tell Colm, Julie and David was that they had bought their mortgages from Bank of Scotland England (BoSE) because Bank of Scotland Ireland (BoSI) no longer existed. This was because in 2010, with debts of over €20 billion, BoSI, a sister company of BoSE, raced back over the Irish Sea to get bailed out by the English taxpayers. The result was a cross-border merger between BoSI and BoSE, all made official by our Mr Justice Peter Kelly. At which point BoSI terminated its trading as a bank in Ireland and struck off its trading company in the Companies Registration Office in Ireland. Sailing back to England debt–free, it morphed into Bank of Scotland plc that is now under the Lloyds Bank umbrella.

How this affects the mortgages of Colm, Julie and David is that BoSI's name was registered as a charge on the title of all borrowers, and under Irish law only the registered charge owner can transfer their charge. So the company must be active in order to transfer their charge, but BoSI had already struck off their trading company and then sold on the loans to vulture companies who bought them for, in some cases, as little as ten cent on the euro.

It was in early 2015 when a question was raised concerning the legitimacy of this transaction that it was brought to the attention of two barristers who were in court trying to get the receiver out of their client's home. Although Ms. Justice Mary Laffoy ruled against the application, she commented that the registration of title raised serious issues for BoSI, who now had more than forty thousand customers.

The next day I was asked if I knew of anyone who might be interested in participating in a test case against BoSI. After putting out the call, I received an email from Jennifer, a thirty-five-year-old mother of four, who had so far been representing herself in court against Tanager, seeking her eviction. The case is due before the court on 24 September 2015. We await the verdict.

The Irish media could no longer sidestep the issue of eviction in Ireland, nor could they ignore the fact that the legal fraternity on behalf of their clients, the banks, often resulted in the banks' customers being made homeless. By March, 118,000 homes were in arrears and of those, 37,400 for two or more years, coupled with the fact that eight thousand cases were going through the courts. Slowly questions began to surface concerning the legality of turning people and their belongings out onto the street with no recourse to the law.

Indeed, had it not been for the nature and background of their first official eviction report, we might assume that it was altruistic motives that caused the Irish media to select the O'Donnell family as their first national case. But in light of the manner with which this family went from obscurity to media fodder overnight, we cannot but suspect that the intention was not to incite national compassion but rather national contempt and in doing so distract from the issue at hand, which was the attempt by a bank with no connection to the O'Donnell family to evict them from their home.

I first met Bruce O'Donnell in a pub in Ringsend one Saturday afternoon in June of 2013. We were at a meeting of Friends of Banking but not of Bankers, which was a group that met monthly to share stories of banking corruption in Ireland. That particular evening one estate agent had shown us invoices from private investigators employed by his former bank to follow him and his wife for two months, photographing and documenting their every move. Bruce himself sat at the end of the table, and as he joined in the conversation we learned that his brother Blake was a solicitor in his father's legal firm, which afforded him access to information that our circle had hitherto been denied. Over the following weeks we kept in contact within the network, exchanging the latest find or query. It was not until Jerry Beades phoned to tell me that the Land League was down in Court 1 supporting the O'Donnells that I realised it was the same man.

Sitting on their side of the bench, Brian, the father, with his son Blake faced a small army of legal professionals acting for Bank of Ireland on the other. Much has been made of their own background in law, and whether or not the emphasis placed on their familiarity with the legal process was misplaced. What is of greater concern is the fact that Mr Judge Kelly, who was the first judge to preside over the case, his registrar had received over one hundred and forty emails from the legal team representing Bank of Ireland, one of which requested Judge Kelly to preside. We cannot but wonder whether there was any connection between this request and the fact that Judge Kelly had purchased a significant amount of shares in Bank of Ireland several years earlier.

The second judge to preside over the case was Mr Justice Brian McGovern, whose first task was to refuse to recuse himself when his wife's connection to a massive building portfolio funded by Bank of Ireland was identified. She was also in court during the same period against the same receiver who had been appointed to the O'Donnell home, all of which was on public record, but the case proceeded nonetheless.

The first point to make about the property of Gorse Hill is that it was an asset of a company in the Isle of Man and had no debt or charge attached to it to the Bank of Ireland plc. It is also worth noting that the O'Donnells did not owe money to Bank of Ireland plc but had taken out their loan with Bank of Ireland Private Banking Ltd, which is a separate registered company. This distinction was shown to the court within the memo of Articles of Association and Charter of the Bank of Ireland, where in the names of directors and secretaries were found to be different to that of Bank of Ireland Private Lending Limited. In spite of which, the Court of Appeal of Ireland ruled that a secretary from a different company can sign on behalf of another separately registered company, one that he/she is not employed by or registered with. Because of this and also due to the fact that no possession order could be legally granted, after Judge McGovern's refusal to recognise the separation between the banks, a receiver was appointed by another bank that had no contractual agreement with the O'Donnells or the Isle of Man company. Disappointingly, the media chose to focus on the size and location of the property rather than the questionable antics of the judges.

Less than two days later the O'Donnells were told to pack up their home and remove all worldly goods. In order to avoid the likelihood of a media circus outside their front door, the whole family departed two hours before the deadline, and Blake and his father made their way to the Bank of Ireland annual general meeting where they threw back the keys to their home. In search of justice, they must now travel to the European Court of Human Rights where it will take years to process their case.

So, if the O'Donnells do not owe money to the bank pursuing them, then what was the purpose of this whole debacle? We can only assume that given the mounting number of lay litigants going before the courts, the bank's intention was to send a clear message through their personal judiciary to the distressed borrowing community that they are the ones holding all the cards. If they can evict a family with whom they have no dealings, then the banking fraternity in Ireland can do what they like.

The story of Hugh and Gráinne is another example of how the Irish banks set about financially ruining their customers through a series of tactical manoeuvres. This includes restricting overdrafts and terminating the discount invoicing facility which is the lifeline of any business. Then there is the demand letter seeking full payment, even though customers are neither in arrears nor have defaulted and full payment cannot be demanded until the banks fulfil their contractual obligations. Regardless of which thousands of developers and businesses across Ireland found themselves victim to this tactic used nationally by the banks, to date no court has questioned this one-sided practice of unconscionable contracts.

Battle worn when we initially met in 2012 at a Friends of Banking but not of Bankers meeting in Dublin West, Hugh and Gráinne were being pursued by the newly formed Irish Bank Resolution Corporation (IBRC), which was the merger between Anglo Irish Bank and Irish Nationwide Building Society, the two biggest cesspits in Ireland's financial sector.

With children aged seven and fourteen months, Hugh and Gráinne ran a successful gastropub which they then mortgaged in order to build a boutique hotel on an adjacent site. Organised by a close family friend, Uncle Liam had been a visitor to their home for over fifteen years as well as attending family celebrations. During the following year they drew down on the loan. With building on schedule and repayments being made on time, there was no reason to assume that the new venture would not thrive.

However, behind the scenes the IBRC was assembling a new team of credit controllers. Handpicked, this group of financial mercenaries had a reputation for leaving their conscience at the door in order to get the job done. Caring nothing for agreements or procedures, it was with threatening behaviour that they extracted as much cash as possible from customers through the selling of assets as well as the family home, and when nothing was left the borrower's corpse would be sold to a vulture company on which to feast (which was often their former friend or colleague). Indeed with a compliant government, a financially indebted judiciary, legal fraternity and media, court registrars double jobbing as sheriffs, and a police force that sees no need for legal documentation, the IBRC hit squad could be assured of full cooperation.

The IBRC credit controllers began their financial assault by reducing Hugh and Gráinne's overdraft, so in order to finish the project a 'roll up everything loan' was organised by their family friend Uncle Liam, who ensured that it became a full commercial loan thereby exempting the family home from protection. At a later date Uncle Liam claimed in his affidavits that he was never in the house attached to the pub nor knew of the existence of Gráinne and her children.

In spite of the fact that the new loan was still under negotiation, a receiver was appointed and soon after that Hugh received a demand letter on a Monday morning for full payment of the entire loan by Friday evening at 5 p.m. By 4 p.m. that Friday the receiver was supervising the drilling of the locks on the business. The interiors were then collected and sold for cents on the euro to Hugh's former competitors. By the end of the following weekend the receiver had stripped the business of its equipment, thereby starving it of any revenue it could have generated. Cash starved, the bank sold everything to satisfy its next fix and in doing so led me to unearth the **biggest robbery in Irish history of €2.5 billion**.

The evidence of this crime was found in the contract between Hugh and Gráinne and the Irish Nationwide Building Society (INBS) in a small, deeply buried but clearly visible paragraph. It read 'on transfer of loan all legal and equitable rights are transferred.' This was irrefutable evidence of the practice of securitisation and would eventually lead to the dismissal of the case against Hugh and Gráinne.

The crime had originated in Irish Nationwide Building Society, whose CEO was Michael Fingleton. Around the corner from INBS Headquarters was Armoin Residential Securities Ltd, which was a private limited company whose function was to securitise all assets belonging to INBS (which means that they were sold on the stock market for a massive return) as well as operating for the purpose of tax avoidance. It is only in hindsight that we can fully appreciate the irony of a company having been set up for the purpose of tax avoidance that upon its own liquidation went on to receive €2.5 billion from the Irish taxpayer themselves.

The normal procedure is that when a company is liquidated, the liquidator makes an inventory of the assets and sells them off. After paying himself, any remaining cash is divided between the creditors, at which point the company is struck off the register in the Companies Registration Office (CRO). It appears, however, that normal procedure did not apply to Armoin Residential Securities Ltd. For upon his appointment as special liquidator, Kieran Wallace (a partner in KPMG) produced the Irish taxpayer's chequebook and wrote a cheque for €2.5 billion to the one shareholder of Armoin Residential Securities Ltd for the full value of their securitised loan book which was €2.5 billion. This was at a time when the Irish markets were being savaged by 50-70 per cent. It is worth noting that KPMG was the last auditing firm for Armoin Residential Securities Ltd.

In other words, KPMG had recently audited Armoin Residential Securities Ltd so they knew how many billions of euro was made in profit from the securitisation of Irish Nationwide Building Society's assets coupled with the fact that virtually no tax was paid. So here was a company making billions of euro from the taxpayer, while paying almost no tax and then receiving a cheque for €2.5 billion from the same taxpayers.

The shareholder of Armoin Residential Securities Ltd is Deutsche International Corporate Services (Ireland) Ltd which is an Irish limited company with an address in Clontarf in Dublin. (KPMG is its auditor.) This same company has billions of euro (taxpayers) invested in Rosneft International

Finance Ltd, which is also an Irish company based at the same
address in Clontarf and is one of the global financing houses
for Rosneft who conduct oil and gas explorations.
Interestingly, the latter produces more oil and gas than Iraq
and Iran combined and has also had international trade
embargos placed. Surprisingly (or not) the director of Armoin
and the director of Deutsche are one and the same person.

Furthermore, KPMG was not the only auditing firm for
Armoin and Irish Nationwide Building Society. Ernst &
Young also audited Irish Nationwide Building Society as well
as Anglo Irish Bank, where in the case of the latter bank they
failed to detect hundreds of millions of euro in concealed loans
given to directors and shareholders of the bank with which
they bought the bank's own shares. Then there was the clean
bill of health that Ernest & Young gave Anglo Irish Bank
regardless of the €7.45 billion overnight deposit from Irish Life
& Permanent, which although pointed out to them, they
claimed that they did not notice.

That's right, in 2008 there was an overnight deposit of €7.45
billion sent to Anglo Irish Bank from Irish Life & Permanent.
For upon learning that Ernst & Young were arriving the
following morning in order to ensure that there was sufficient
liquidity and that the books balanced, 'a call went out' from
Anglo Irish Bank for €7.45 billion. Irish Life & Permanent
(whose auditors were KPMG at that time) answered the call
and ensured that €7.45 billion was transferred in time for the
auditors' inspection. In doing so, they became party to the
criminal act of falsification of the accounts as well as the
manipulation of Anglo Irish Bank share values that ended up
conning a nation and investors across the world.

At this point it is worth remembering that it was our own
bondholder Minister for Finance Michael Noonan who was
responsible for appointing KPMG as special liquidator to

IBRC; the same minister who also sanctioned the dropping of a civil legal case against a former director of Irish Nationwide Building Society that had involved €29.3 million. In other words, our Minister for Finance interfered with the duties of the Director of Public Prosecution which resulted in that director's case being dropped.

To this day the Irish taxpayer funds the pensions of the same directors who were responsible for the policies of austerity. Directors like Michael Fingleton who in addition to the €28 million personal pension fund paid for by Irish Nationwide Building Society in 2007 also remunerated himself to the tune of €10 million from the period the property bubble began inflating on 1 January 2003 until his departure on 30 April 2009. Then there was the €1 million pre-contractual bonus he paid himself in 2008. Also, let us not forget how former Anglo Irish Bank chairman Seán FitzPatrick split his €3.7 million pension with his wife Catriona so that €1.85 million was put out of the reach of creditors. Finally there is the case of the missing €6 billion that was securitised, as stated on the Anglo Tapes of September 2008. The question is how much money was made from this money and by whom? More importantly, the taxpayers of Ireland would like to know where all this money is now.

Furthermore, IBRC sold American loans with a face value of $8.6 billion at a discount of 80 cent in the euro. The loan sale netted the IBRC about €5 billion in cash. Bidders included Deutsche Bank. Days after the sale, IBRC paid €1.25 billion to senior unguaranteed, unsecured bondholders and to date no one has named the recipients of these billions of taxpayers' euro.

Unless we are in any doubt of the endemic corruption in the Irish banking system, let us remember how Anglo Irish Bank signed off on a multimillion euro loan extension for a foreign property company that was co-owned by its former chief executive Seán FitzPatrick on the same day that it was taken into State ownership by the liquidator KPMG. This loan was for €14.6 million with a further €2.6 million on 21 January, 2009 – the very day legislation nationalising the troubled lender was enacted. Records reveal the company subsequently drew down almost €17 million of the total €17.2 million. Some of the money was used for the purchase of a €10.25 million villa on the French Riviera and €450,000 in real estate agent fees. However, it is not yet known what the rest of the money was spent on.

In Hugh and Gráinne's case they had borrowed money from Irish Nationwide which was then securitised by Armoin. Then came the crash and the Irish taxpayer paid 100 per cent of the loan books of Anglo, Irish Nationwide and Armoin, all of which morphed into IBRC. Subsequently, on 2 April 2014 the newly formed IBRC sold on its loan books again to American vulture companies like Lone Star and Oaktree Capital. In which case Irish Nationwide were paid three times, first of all by the securitisation process, secondly by the taxpayers and then by the vulture companies, not forgetting the manipulation of interest which should be called what it is, theft. The banks stole money from families by overcharging interest in the knowledge that in less than a year many of these same families would be unemployed because of the banks' own criminal actions.

A far cry from Fingleton's Mediterranean lifestyle, Hugh and Gráinne had an eviction order waiting to be executed when with the help of forensic accountants they discovered that they had been overcharged by €1.4 million. On production of the evidence, they assumed that the judge would dismiss the case, after all they could not have been accused of defaulting if they had had the money that was stolen from them by the same bank that was now pursuing them. But Ireland's justice-less courts were to strike again, this time at the hands of Mr Justice Kelly who had spent the previous two years signing one eviction order after another. A devout Catholic who dines with bishops and enjoys a lavish apartment metres away from his beloved Papa in Vatican City, Judge Kelly openly professes his devotion with pontiff cufflinks, whilst his registrar's online dealings with the banks' legal teams go unreported.

Therefore, when Hugh and Gráinne found themselves standing in front of Judge Kelly they might have expected a level of compassion. Perhaps reference would be made to the Eighth Commandment considering that the bank had stolen from them. Instead they were shouted at in front of a packed courtroom. 'You got the money,' Judge Kelly roared and without hesitation dismissed the €1.4 million of over-charging/robbery.

'You owe €24 million so deduct €1.4 million, actually let's round it off to €21 million you owe.'

In spite of their protests Judge Kelly granted possession of Hugh and Gráinne's home. Although his decision was appealed to the Supreme Court the eviction still went ahead. It appears that only in Ireland can an appeal be made to the highest court in the land and yet an order can be executed prior to the hearing that appeal. Their eviction was scheduled for 6 June at five o'clock.

At the last minute Gráinne brought an emergency application before the court seeking to stay the eviction order of Judge Kelly. Ordinarily this action would have had little or no effect upon the course of events but this time would be different.

Instead of taking their place in litigation against Hugh and Gráinne, counsel for the IBRC sought to have the vulture fund named. In support of which, they presented an affidavit claiming that their client had transferred its legal and equitable rights, so the same bank that had sold all its loans in a very public way was now claiming no right to them. The reason they decided to come clean was perhaps that they had no choice as their loan books would have shown that they had sold on all their legal and equitable rights and on what date this had occurred. After traumatising a family for six years, depleting every cent they had and causing Hugh to suffer a heart attack brought on by the stress, it appeared that the IBRC confessed that they did not even own the loan for which they were pursuing them. Indeed such had become this couple's fear of eviction that the day following Hugh's open heart surgery he insisted on attending court. Regardless of the numerous letters written by his cardiologist advising against it, the judge was having none of it and ordered him to attend. So sitting in his wheelchair with Gráinne by this side, Hugh's counsel requested an adjournment in spite of the legal team for the IBRC claiming that his illness was exaggerated and insisting that they proceed. Hugh got one week's adjournment, just seven days to recuperate.

The end result was that the Supreme Court referred the case back to the new Court of Appeal where the Bank's request was dismissed and Hugh and Gráinne were left with no named plaintiff. The IBRC, in claiming it had no legal right, left the vulture company with a mountain of litigation ahead of them and no valid order to evict. No doubt we have not heard the last of these cases and wait to see how a vulture company seeks to enforce a contract it bought for 20 per cent of the value from a bank that received 100 per cent of the value multiple times and then again from the taxpayers of Ireland.

I learned more about these activities directly from whistleblowers themselves, many of whom had been retired early in an effort to cosmetically remove any perceived blemishes on the good name of the post-boom banks. However, regardless of the decades behind them, their craving for power had not diminished over time and with their trough of victims now dried up they were seeking a new well from which to feed. Mostly they were middle-aged men who had betrayed their position of trust from the outset; my latest gamekeeper-turned-poacher was eager to meet me. Referring to a person who turns on their own, Edward had retired from the Bank of Ireland with a pension that would support a small football team. Not content to pass away his twilight years with a family he did not know or a wife he hardly spoke to, he intended instead to continue doing what he did best, destroying the lives of hard-working people, one of whom I had comforted the previous year as she tried to make sense of her husband's death by self-administered rat poison, driven by the mental torture brought on by the same individual I was about to meet.

In February 2014, standing across the road from a hotel in Cork, I watched Edward seated comfortably inside. Hoping to use my list of distressed bank customers to fund his new 'financial enterprise', I, on the other hand, intended to use it to gain his trust and in doing so learn about the inner dealings of the banking system. Aware that I had the names of more than two thousand people who needed financial advice, Edward intended to offer them various financial packages such as loan restructuring or a new mortgage, which would remove a bad loan for his friends. Now renamed, it would look like new lending for the bank, for which he would receive a healthy commission.

I was greeted with an outstretched hand.

'Tom Darcy?' he asked.

'Edward,' I replied, 'so nice to meet you.'

With his green farmer's jacket, worn jeans and tired, brown leather bag, he opened his pitch by telling me of his vast experience in treasury and lending with Bank of Ireland. According to their own policy, they did not register most of their commercial loans in the Companies Registration Office, in spite of the fact that it is mandatory to do so by law within twenty-one days. Fishing as to whether I was aware of their reason, I surmised that it was probably because the loan had been already sold on.

'It's all in the paperwork, Tom,' my gamekeeper-turned-poacher laughed, 'or lack thereof.'

It appeared that my whistleblower, in offering me an olive branch from a poisonous tree, had inadvertently handed me the stick with which I could beat the banks black and blue. I was then asked about the people on my books. Slowly reaching into my briefcase, I lifted out a book with two thousand names, bound in a black cover entitled 'Families'. A quick glance was enough to lull my whistleblower into a false sense of security that loosened his tongue even more.

Like a soldier recounting his days in battle, Edward had a strange view of his own history. For a battle implies equality of force, armament and number, whereas no such equality ever existed between his financial army and the landowners whose financial ruin he orchestrated. Listening attentively, I heard of how in the 1980s a public spectacle was made of the farmers who fell on hard times. Driven to bankruptcy and eviction by the banks, local newspapers would then be used to spread the story.

'Didn't matter how much money it cost them,' Edward laughed, 'the fuckers would sell their firstborn to keep us happy back then.'

As our conversation came to an end, he reached out his hand. 'We'll make millions out of this, Tom, fuckin' millions.'

It was, however, a man calling himself Slim Shady whose remarkable knowledge of banking and absence of integrity showed me how a small number of individuals can bring a country to its knees.

Due to his vocabulary resembling more my sons' than mine, I assumed that my latest whistleblower was a young guy whose conscience had got the better of him. Sadly, my expectations could not have been further from the truth.

We met soon after our first phone call in the Gresham Hotel, in Dublin, at his request. Expecting a twenty-something with jeans hanging down over his shorts and bright trainers offset with a baseball cap, it was soon apparent it was my whistleblower's slight frame that accounted for his self-appointed nickname with the shady part referring to his dealings. There was no resemblance to the Eminem song of the same name.

'Tom Darcy?' I turned around.

'I'm Slim Shady'. Sitting down, my Middle-Aged Banker proceeded to tell me about his 'muppets' and how 'we hook 'em and gut them'.

'You mean your customers?' I asked.

'Our muppets,' I was corrected.

'Firstly, we target a business with about fifty staff and plenty of equity in the warehouse or factory with little debt attached to it. The owner has a couple of hundred thousand in overdrafts secured on the premises. Tucked in the small print are all his assets including his home. We then start to reduce the overdraft, and when he thinks he will lose the business, we turn the overdraft into a loan, which his wife also signs as co-director of the company.'

Slim Shady put his hand in the air and imitated hitting a nail with a hammer.

'Bang, that nail is in the coffin,' he laughed. 'It doesn't matter if he is paying his loan, we continue to reduce the overdrafts so he can't operate his business and BANG he's gone, but that's not the best part.' My whistleblower sat bolt upright and stared me in the face.

'Getting his wife to co-sign means that the family home is no longer protected by law nor are their constitutional rights. Then we take the overdraft money and put it into our balance sheets making us look good, appoint a receiver, fire sale anything of value, including his factories and then go after his home.' It appeared that Slim Shady was living up to his username.

'What about the employees, their families and their homes? Doesn't it bother you?' I asked, trying to remain calm.

'It's business, that's all. You can't take it personally, that's the job.'

I knew that what my whistleblower was saying was correct as my good friend Peter had experienced similar tactics with his bank. Although servicing his overdraft every month, it was nonetheless reduced over time and then converted into a loan. After only a month the bank wrongly claimed that Peter was defaulting and sent an agent to inform his customers of his financial problems, making them seek alternative suppliers after thirty-six years' trading. Twenty-three people were made unemployed and the bank appointed a receiver who sold everything at fire sale. They then came after Peter's home, and since his wife had co-signed on the loan it was claimed as a commercial loan bypassing all rights the wife had under the Family Home Protection Act 1976.

I sat stunned. 'How do you sleep at night?' I asked.

'That's the game,' smiled my whistleblower, 'there are winners and losers. You can't win when we hold all the cards.'

Hardly able to contain my rage I demanded to know why he was telling me all this if he held all the cards. Mr Shady sat back comfortably. 'So that you know the bank will always win. We are in charge of this country because we control the money. The judges do what we tell them because they're scared we will come after their homes too and government ministers are only thinking about their pensions and payoffs.

They're not going to stop us.' He laughed again. 'They can't.'

By this stage I was shaking with anger. 'I'm losing my home because of bastards like you,' I spat out, as my voice filled the Gresham Hotel. Visibly flustered, Slim Shady ran out.

The following month I was in the North Star Hotel in Dublin City waiting for Harry, another potential whistle-blower. Having just sat down, I felt a tapping on my shoulder. Turning around, I saw a tall man in his early sixties indicating for me to follow him. Exiting the hotel doors, we took a left, heading away from the city and eventually turning into a side lane.

'I shouldn't be doing this,' whispered Harry under his breath. 'I have a family and my daughter is pregnant; it could destroy them.'

Trying to reassure him, I confirmed that I was also a father. 'I was with another father last Thursday,' I went on to say, 'except it was his funeral. He left a pregnant wife and a two-year-old daughter behind. He couldn't take the threats from the banks any more.'

Then, from under his coat, Harry pulled out a bundle of Ulster Bank statements from customer accounts. Although in arrears, they all had credit entries of €6,000–€8,000 in their accounts.

'How is that possible?' I asked, 'if they are not working?'

It turned out that Ulster Bank was directly applying to the Irish Revenue Commissioners for their customers' mortgage relief and then crediting the same amount to the customers' account.

'We have being doing this for years,' Harry explained, 'and I know two other banks doing the same. There are up to forty thousand similar accounts. It's what we jokingly call our "back-door bailout".'

I went on to learn how the Irish banks were charging borrowers up to 2,000 per cent interest.

'We all know that the banks got bailed out,' my whistle-blower continued, 'but what people don't realise is that the European Central Bank interest rates to banks are 0.025 per cent, but our banks are charging borrowers up to 5 per cent. My bank is adding an average of 85 per cent, which is profit, and then showing it as arrears.'

Thinking of the homeowners being dragged into court with arrears of even €100,000, the truth is that they are only in arrears of €15,000. The rest is profit for the bank, who then gets possession of the house, kicks out the family, sells it at a fire sale and claims all their losses, which includes hidden profit.

Within twenty-four hours I had received bank statements from my Facebook friends confirming Harry's claim. The bank was indeed claiming a back-door bailout. For added assurance I had recorded the interview and played it to a journalist from the *Irish Independent*. Her shock was obvious, but I never heard from her again. Then I contacted a former treasury banker to confirm Harry's claim about interest rates. As he explained, the ECB were lending at the figures Harry had claimed and the Irish banks were then charging taxpayers 2000 per cent for the money the taxpayer paid and continues to pay in the bailout for which the banks had no expenditure.

In hindsight, there is no doubt that without my whistle-blowers I would have had only pieces of the whole story. Still now, a couple of times per month, these brave individuals send me information from the highest ranks of our governmental, legal and financial institutions that allows me to piece together the jigsaw in its entirety. At this point there is no need to dwell on the treachery of certain individuals in positions of responsibility and how their premeditated acts of betrayal towards their own citizens have effectively brought our country to the verge of collapse, but instead accept the picture that the jigsaw is revealing and decide what we are going to do about it.

7

The Government Knew Everything

The following information was revealed to me in early May 2015. Received from one of my whistleblowers, it not only proves the toxic relationship between the Government and the financial sector, but how this toxicity has been allowed to seep into the home of every Irish citizen. As the curtain is pulled back and the truth revealed, let us take a moment to remember those who continue to suffer as a result of the corruption of those we trusted: the marriages that broke up, the children who lost a parent and the Irish men and women who could not take any more pressure and took their own lives.

It could be said that no discussion about corruption within the Irish financial sector would be complete without reference to Seán FitzPatrick, former head of Anglo Irish Bank. What he did and did not do filled newspapers for months; we heard about his management style, where the absence of minutes during even the most important meetings have made it impossible to piece together the full extent of the loans made to friends.

Indeed there are many things that we will never understand about the Seán FitzPatrick/Anglo debacle that stole hundreds of millions of euro in shares from unsuspecting customers whose only mistake (if it could be called that) was trusting those in positions of power. However, to assume that

the truth can be found within the walls of the Anglo Irish
Bank building is a distraction, rather we need to go to Kildare
Street, to our Government offices.

Let us begin in May 2015 when I received information
pertaining to the criminal case against Seán FitzPatrick that
was to take place the following day. It predicted that the case
would not proceed, given that on 8 May the main witness in
the Office of the Director of Corporate Enforcement had
signed himself into the psychiatric unit of Saint John of God
Hospital, which allowed him to avoid standing over an
affidavit he had been working on for months with the Director
of Public Prosecutions. Strange, given that the witness was
only responsible for bringing the evidence to the attention of
the Director of Public Prosecutions, one wonders why the case
was dropped. After all, it was the Director of Public
Prosecution's responsibility to prosecute, and it was the
balance sheet of Anglo Irish Bank that provided the evidence
by showing the discrepancies of between €20 million to €30
million. So why did it matter where the witness was residing?

But, no, the case was dropped, and Seán FitzPatrick
returned to his opulent lifestyle courtesy of the Irish taxpayer.
And were it not for the courage of my whistleblower deep
inside Dáil Éireann, the Irish people would have been left
assuming that the unavailability of the 'messenger' was the
reason behind this outcome. However, now we can put
forward another reason why Seán FitzPatrick has never been
prosecuted nor probably ever will be by revealing the true
events of the night of 30 September 2008, to which he himself
may have also been privy.

First of all let us return to November 2007 when, in light
of the subprime crisis in the USA, the Irish Minister for
Finance commissioned a five-hundred page report, which was
referred to in the Department of Finance as 'The Financial

Doomsday Book' on the state of the Irish banks. As it turned out, the Irish banks were insolvent, which means that they contravened their legislated obligation to deposit securities with the Central Bank of Ireland in respect of its loan to deposit ratios and liquidity ratios under the Central Bank Acts of 1942–1989. As a result, the Irish banks were unable to renew their banking licence in accordance with statute law.

On 8 February 2008 the report was received and a week later on the 15th every Irish bank entered into a contractual agreement with the Central Bank. The agreement was that in exchange for recapitalisation, the banks pledged all their present and future profits and assets. That night, every bank in Ireland ticked the insolvent box and declared that they were insolvent/bankrupt or unable to pay creditors, and yet they still got the money.

The contract was called a C1 Registered Mortgage Document and was stamped in the Companies Registration Office (CRO) on 15 February but was not made public for another four months, which denied every shareholder and account holder in every bank in Ireland the opportunity to sell their shares and recoup at least some of their life savings.

Sixteen weeks after the C1 Registered Mortgage Document was identified on the CRO website, on 30 September 2008 the CEOs of the principal banks in Ireland met at midnight with the Minister for Finance and the Taoiseach demanding a guarantee. A blanket guarantee of the banks' liabilities was issued overnight.

Eleven weeks after the guarantee was given the financial institutions returned their financial records to the CRO for the benefit of the shareholders, it read that **some** of the assets had been pledged but not *all*, which we now know was a complete lie and resulted in the financial ruination of a country. In the absence of transparency a further document called the Liquidity Document, which was attached to the C1 Registered Mortgage Document, has never been located.

So, let us recap on what we think happened in 2008 and what really did happen. We, the Irish people, were led to believe that our Government knew nothing about our bankrupt banks until 29/30 September 2008. Citing a regulator asleep at the helm, a corrupt head of Anglo Irish Bank (which I am not disputing) and a Government negligent in its duties may at first appear to be strong and serious allegations. However, the possibility of negligence pales in comparison to the act of treason when we now know that for almost a year previously the Government knew that every bank in Ireland was insolvent and therefore any trading, issuing of loans or mortgages or conducting of any financial business on the stock exchange was illegal.

The Irish people had been well and truly lied to by both the banks and then the Government who claimed that they had acted in our best interest by issuing the guarantee. To deflect from their treachery, they then turned the finger on hard-working men and women who they accused of 'partying too hard', and as a result of which 'the good times were over'. Since then the Government has done nothing to help Irish citizens facing homelessness but have continued to support the banks in their illegal activities – because it is important to remember that the banks are still insolvent and the Government still knows that.

8

Epilogue

The relationship between various individuals, political party members, members of financial institutions and the judiciary have already been discussed in relation to their involvement in using taxpayers' money to generate billions of euro from the process of securitisation. It appears that the ink is barely dry on loan agreements when they are sold on, which returns the lender their stake as well as a handsome profit. They also receive the interest on something they no longer hold but continue to manipulate (steal) when the legal and equitable rights are transferred.

Then there is the Irish taxpayers' chequebook that was produced to fund a company in liquidation to the tune of €2.5 billion. This money went on to create billions more euro from which we have not benefitted. It certainly appears that the Irish citizen is the 'go to person' for a group of individuals when money is needed to be made.

However with reference to the current controversy that is Irish Water, it seems that the billions of euro created from the selling and reselling of our loans fall short of the financial requirements of Ireland's cabal, who have now resorted to acquiring payment for a service for which we already pay for twice. Currently we are being required to pay again, this time to a company whose purchase was facilitated by the taxpayers' bailed-out bank AIB.

In short, Denis O'Brien (listed amongst the world's top two hundred billionaires in 2015), as a result of personal loans and securities to Anglo Irish Bank, owed €833.3 million to the Irish taxpayer, regardless of the fact that he has a net worth of €6.8 billion. For one of his companies he received a write-down of €140 million. Then Colm Doherty in AIB organised the purchase price of €47.5 million which allowed Denis O'Brien to buy Siteserv, a company that had already received a €100 million write-down. In other words, the Irish taxpayer facilitated the initial write-down for Siteserv. We then purchased the same company that will facilitate the taxation of this generation and generations to come for the supply of water.

In 2006 Siteserv plc (contractor for Irish Water that installs water meters), represented by Davy Stockbrokers, raised almost €10.5 million from its flotation on Dublin's IEX market. Six years later it was reported that Siteserv would be sold at a 'significant discount to its bank debt of 150 million'. Davy Stockbrokers and KPMG would handle the sale.

17 March 2012, it was reported that IBRC agreed to write off €100 million of the approximate debt of €150 million owed by Siteserv footed by the taxpayers of Ireland. Twelve days later An Taoiseach Enda Kenny appeared at the New York Stock Exchange with Denis O'Brien. Ten days later Mr O'Brien and Irish Minister for the Environment Phil Hogan said: 'In due course, Siteserv will, no doubt, tender for state contracts, such as, for example, the installation of water meters at households around the country – a contract that will be granted by the Department of the Environment.' We must remember that Minister Phil Hogan snubbed an offer by Siemens to finance water meters which would have resulted in a saving for the taxpayer of €350 million. Siemens offered to foot the €810 million-plus cost of

installing meters in 1.3 million Irish homes on 15 April 2012, but no, the Irish Government preferred to pay Mr O'Brien from the public coffers at a time when public services were in dire need of investment.

On 8 December 2013, Denis O'Brien gains full control of Topaz and former Taoiseach Brian Cowen as well as former managing director of AIB, Colm Doherty, are appointed to the boards of Topaz and Siteserv.

IBRC also wrote off €64 million for Blue Ocean Associates, another O'Brien-owned company as well as €65 million for his Beacon Hospital in Sandyford, County Dublin. In total, Denis O'Brien received over €300 million in write-offs, all admittedly paid for by Irish taxpayers. According to the Moriarty Tribunal, he paid and bribed Government ministers and is not even a tax resident in Ireland, despite enslaved Irish taxpayers paying for his private jet and mansion in the Bahamas. What does Denis O'Brien do for them in return?

What about my own story?
June 2015
Clare and I sat together for the third time in seven months awaiting Mr Justice Keane's decision to either grant possession of our home to AIB for the second time in three years or grant us a full hearing. Before our case is heard, we witness Judge Keane's admonishment of yet another lay litigant. Mid-forties, wearing an old brown suit and carrying eight A4 pages, the man requested the digital recordings of his case attended weeks earlier. In doing so, he highlighted the latest myth of legislative change introduced two years earlier that claims to give both parties equal access to digital recordings of court proceedings.

First of all, these recordings are never required by the banks as their team of juniors record every word and note every reaction made. Unlike the lay litigant who, while doing the work of three people, often forgets most of what was said and as a result, must now bring more motions to court which costs his week's sustenance of €188. The defendant presents his case, reciting the rules of the European Convention on Human Rights regarding his right to a fair trial. My heart sinks. He may as well be reciting from the telephone directory for all the good it will do. Finally, Judge Keane grants a recordings to be released at the cost of €800, citing that he would not burden the taxpayer with the expense. Becoming irritated at the man's insistence that his right to justice is being denied and that his only crime is to be penniless, Judge Keane reiterates his ruling. With justice unobtainable, this man is merely another Irish citizen whose constitutional rights are violated, unlike those who commit heinous crimes and are given counsel and costs to guarantee that their constitutional rights are upheld.

As my case number is called, I open my notebook. Scribbling on the top of the page, predicting the judge's verdict, I write 'Refused', at which point Judge Keane goes on to refute each claim made by me, adding authorities for the benefit of the bank's counsel. He then refers to Clare's affidavit and dismisses her claim that we lived as a family in Woodview, in Howth, before the contracts were signed, even though the Supreme Court already iterated this point at length. For the second time in three years, possession of our family home is given by a judge who considers that justice is best served by denying justice. That evening, the fear that had haunted us both now returns, knowing that once again we would be **waiting for the sheriff.**

Appendices

APPENDIX A

TDs That Voted in Favour of the Land and Conveyancing Law Reform Bill 2013

Here is a list of the TDs that voted to evict your family, neighbours and friends and who care nothing for the lost lives and desecration of families across this country of Ireland.

See is your local TD here:

Breen, Pat	Creighton, Lucinda	Harris, Simon
Bruton, Richard	Daly, Jim	Hayes, Brian
Butler, Ray	Deasy, John	Heydon, Martin
Buttimer, Jerry	Deenihan, Jimmy	Hogan, Phil
Byrne, Catherine	Deering, Pat	Howlin, Brendan
Byrne, Eric	Doherty, Regina	Humphreys, Heather
Cannon, Ciarán	Donnelly, Stephen S	Humphreys, Kevin
Carey, Joe	Donohoe, Paschal	Keating, Derek
Coffee, Paudie	Doyle, Andrew	Kehoe, Paul
Collins, Áine	Durkan, Bernard J	Kelly, Alan
Conaghan, Michael	English, Damien	Kenny, Seán
Conlan, Seán	Feighan, Frank	Kyne, Seán
Connaughton, Paul J	Fitzgerald, Frances	Lawlor, Anthony
Conway, Ciara	Fitzpatrick, Peter	Lynch, Ciarán
Coonan, Noel	Flanagan, Charles	Lynch, Kathleen
Corcoran Kennedy, Marcella	Gilmore, Eamonn	Lyons, John
	Griffin, Brendan	McCarthy, Michael
Costello, Joe	Hannigan, Dominic	McEntree, Helen
Creed, Michael	Harrington, Noel	McGinley, Dinny

167

McHugh, Joe   Neville, Dan   Rabbitte, Pat
McLoughlin, Tony   Noonan, Michael   Reilly, James
McNamara, Michael   Ó Ríordáin, Aodhán   Ryan, Brendan
Maloney, Eamon   O'Donnell, Kieran   Shatter, Alan
Matthews, Peter   O'Donovan, Patrick   Spring, Arthur
Mitchell, Olivia   O'Dowd, Fergus   Stagg, Emmet
Mitchell O'Connor,   O'Mahony, John   Stanton, David
   Mary   O'Reilly, Joe   Tuffy, Joanna
Mulherin, Michelle   O'Sullivan, Jan   Wall, Jack
Murphy, Dara   Perry, John   Walsh, Brian
Murphy, Eoghan   Phelan, Ann   White, Alex
Nash, Gerald   Phelan, John Paul

To the above TDs: Our Constitution promotes the common good with due observance of prudence, justice and charity, so that the dignity and freedom of the individual may be assured, true social order attained, the unity of our country restored and concord established with other nations.

Article 41.3.1° – The State pledges itself to guard with special care the institution of Marriage, on which the Family is founded.

Article 45.4.1° – The State pledges itself to safeguard with special care the economic interests of the weaker sections of the community.

Voting in favour of a bill that evicts and destroys innocent families in this State is contrary to the above.

Minister Richard Bruton, Minister for Jobs, Enterprise and Innovation, here is an idea: let us pass a Bill that allows bankers to evict innocent families from their homes. But why would Minister Bruton care when he earns over €300,000 per year and has a pension for the rest of his life?

Jerry Buttimer, TD: The consequence of eviction is not only the destruction of families but mental health issues. Stop the inhumane persecution of the people you claim to represent. By saying and doing nothing to support them, you prove that you do not give a damn.

Catherine Byrne, TD is the former Lord Mayor of Dublin and claims to be a spokesperson for the elderly. Many of the same elderly are now providing a home for their children and grandchildren. These are often the same elderly who went guarantor for their adult children and now live in fear of the banks pursuing them and the sheriff arriving at their door.

Michael Noonan, TD: To the people of Limerick, the coffin that you follow may be due to Michael Noonan's disregard for his countrymen and women by voting in a law that makes whole families homeless.

Ciarán Lynch, TD pledged to 'Take a Step for Simon' (Simon Community). At a briefing on 4 October 2012, he was told about homelessness in his constituency and the pressure on his local Simon Community, but nine months later he voted in favour of a Bill that would increase homelessness. 'I work tirelessly on behalf of hard-working families and their communities to support future growth and prosperity in the Cork area. If I am re-elected by the people of Cork South-Central in the upcoming election, I will redouble my efforts on their behalf to prevent a further drop in the quality of people's lives.' Upon election by you, the electorate Ciarán got his €100,000 salary plus expenses of €40,000 per annum.

Alan Shatter, TD has the largest property portfolio of any member of Ireland's Government. He is no stranger to evicting people. Cliff Goldstein, a retired school guidance counsellor, faced eviction from his home following legal action by the former Justice Minister Alan Shatter and his wife, Carol. Alan Shatter's support for the Land and Conveyancing Law Reform Bill 2013 will generate billions of euro for legal firms who evict families, paid for by the taxpayer.

Joe O'Reilly, TD: Who is Joe representing – his constituents or the banks? Joe supported a Bill that gives statute laws to criminal bankers who to date have not been made accountable for their actions. Joe also supported a retroactive law which is contrary to our Constitution.

Phil Hogan, TD: Minister Phil Hogan had an interest-free mortgage on his house in Haddington Square, which is valued at €1 million as well as a penthouse in Portugal. Furthermore, Phil Hogan's interest-free loans came through Irish Nationwide boss Michael Fingleton.

Eamonn Gilmore, TD: With over €6000 per week going into the Gilmore household, Eamonn claims that he did not get his wife a €117,000 job in the Department of Education and Skills. Eamonn Gilmore is paid €200,000 per year plus expenses and he and his wife will receive a pension of over €200,000 for the rest of their lives. Indeed, Mrs Gilmore received €525,000 for a school site that is now valued at €100,000. Eamonn Gilmore also has four advisors costing €500,000 per year compared to an average couple who are in the insolvency programme and receive €161 per week to pay bills, food and provide for their children's needs. They have committed no crimes, broken no laws and yet are treated as criminals. It is like penal servitude imposed on a nation's people by those who lead Hollywood lifestyles.

Eamonn Maloney, TD: 'Opposition members use emotive language and words such as *eviction* for purely political gain. This is reprehensible and indicates a mentality that is not interested in solving the crisis. We must realise that the mortgage crisis comes in different levels and therefore it requires a multi-faceted response. There are also physical and psychological effects, particularly if there are children in the household. It can be a difficult and traumatic experience for all members of the family.' Eamonn should check the meaning of the word *hypocrite*, especially when his solution appears to be to evict families across the country.

Member of the Irish Farmers' Association and human rights officer, Michael McNamara, TD voted in favour of evicting his fellow farming families. Contact Michael McNamara and express your disgust at his actions and demand that he revokes his support for the Land and Conveyancing Law Reform Act 2013 or resign.

Damien English, TD: 'I love spending time with my family. I'm married to Laura and we have two young children (Harvey, two, and Karla, seven months). They're at a great age now and in between the teething we have great fun with them.' What about the families in his own constituency who faced eviction? Damien English will knock on your door shortly for your support for his colleagues in elections. Please do to him as he does to his neighbours: evict him from your doorstep.

Seán Kyne, TD enabled families to obtain an Irish death certificate for loved ones who died abroad whilst at the same time signing into law a Bill that causes mental anguish to the Irish in their own homes. However, will Seán Kyne get those lost souls' death certificates and write 'I am sorry'? To the people of Galway, please do not support Seán Kyne or his party in future elections. Contact Seán Kyne and demand that he revoke his support for a Bill that is destroying innocent families across Ireland.

Lucinda Creighton, TD: She calls for the protection of the rights of the unborn but appears unconcerned with the children who are currently suffering from homelessness. Contact Lucinda and demand that she revokes her support for a Bill that discards children from their homes. Where is her compassion for the families suffering tonight and every night?

Brian Hayes, MEP said that the Land and Conveyancing Law Reform Bill 'had nothing to do with eviction', which means that either he is lying or does not understand the content of a Bill he signed. Is this the type of person you want representing you?

Áine Collins, TD: Definition of conscience: noun: conscience; plural noun: consciences; behaviour; He/she had a guilty conscience about his/her desires; synonyms: sense of right and wrong, sense of right, moral sense, still small voice, inner voice, voice within. Contact Áine Collins and demand that she revokes her support for the Land and Conveyancing Law Reform Bill or resign from her €2,000 a week job while children are made homeless by her lack of conscience.

Joe Costello, TD: Minister for Trade and Development launched a school rehabilitation programme in Uganda and yet voted to close Irish schools and increase class sizes. Then he voted to evict families.

Eoghan Murphy, TD says 'No' to property tax but 'Yes' to eviction. The Dublin South East TD said property tax is 'grossly unfair' and called on Mr Noonan to make it fairer before its introduction. However, Eoghan thinks putting families onto the road is acceptable and the trauma that follows in its wake.

Joanna Tuffy, TD is a homewrecker named and shamed! To every mother in Ireland, please ask Joanna Tuffy why she voted for a Bill that forces families apart. Mothers, wipe away the tears of your children that suffer this nightmare as you watch your family torn apart.

Ray Butler, TD is a father of four children who clearly cares nothing for your children's needs. Let us remind him of what our Constitution says to do: 'Promote the common good, with due observance of Prudence, Justice and Charity, so that the dignity and freedom of the individual may be assured, true social order attained, the unity of our country restored, and concord established with other nations.' To all in Trim: This is the calibre of representative you have. Tens of thousands of childhoods are being destroyed, thousands of people will take their own lives, and all because Ray Butler could not honour our Constitution, his oath of office and his election promises.

Peter Fitzpatrick, TD said that he will not vacate his seat in the Dáil if there are further cuts to Louth County Hospital. Peter Fitzpatrick is not respectful to the tens of thousands of families suffering every day in this country: the children, mothers, tormented souls who all suffer as a result of his actions.

Ciara Conway, TD: According to Ciara, the solution to improving child welfare is to remove children from their homes. Ciara Conway is TD for Waterford and vice chairperson of the Oireachtas Committee on Health and Children.

Ciara addresses challenges faced by lone parents:

1. How to stop being evicted from my home? Ciara voted to evict them.
2. How to feed my children? Ciara voted to cut allowances in the Budget.
3. How to keep my children warm? Ciara voted to reduce fuel allowance.
4. How to find integrity, honesty, loyalty in a Labour TD? LOL

Michael McCarthy, TD had a mother removed from his constituency office for protesting against cuts that affected the welfare of her autistic child. In 2011 he stated that 'we need a Constitution that will protect our children and guide the courts to make decisions that will keep families together and value their rights.' Seriously?

Regina Doherty, TD: Named but not ashamed. Meath East TD Regina Doherty could face prosecution by the Office of the Director of Corporate Enforcement. A creditors' meeting to put her business into liquidation was held in 2013. Losses were understood to be €280,000, including almost €60,000 owed to the Revenue Commissioners and €50,000 owed to State-owned bank AIB. (No enforcement followed.)

1. More community-based Gardaí. Regina voted to close Garda Stations.
2. Class sizes reduced to 20/1. Regina voted for a budget that increased class sizes 30/1.
3. Increased local amenities in our towns. Regina voted for a 40 per cent increase in excise duties costing over 3,000 jobs and forced hard-pressed pubs, hotels and restaurants to close.

Regina's letter to her constituents during the local elections read: 'I believe you deserve the right to an affordable home, have your rights respected and to have your dignity'. Regina, where is the dignity in being dragged out of your home as your children watch and you're left like rubbish on the street? There is no possibility of affordable homes when criminal bankers refuse to accept open-market values of properties to restructure agreements. Instead they pay billions of euro of taxpayers' money to solicitors' firms to evict families.

Noel Harrington, TD: Like other TDs, Noel claims over €1,000 in expenses per week. In 2012, TDs in Cork claimed €1 million in expenses in total. Topping the list, Noel Harrington claimed over €63,500, which is over €1,300 per week, and then there is his salary of €100,000. Michael Collins would turn in his grave to witness his rebel county's so-called representatives voting in favour of evicting families.

Pat Deering, TD called on lenders to pass on mortgage cuts. On 8 July 2012, he said that 'people with big mortgages are under enormous pressure'. So Pat's solution is clearly to extend further laws to criminal bankers to evict those same people. Pat welcomes news that household charge passes the 50 per cent mark. He is clearly happy that you are being taxed to death.

Stephen Donnelly, TD.

This letter was sent to Stephen Donnelly and Pat Kenny. Neither replied.

Stephen,

With reference to your article in the *Sunday Independent*, I am both confused and saddened at your public stance. If you visit my Facebook page, Tom Darcy Eviction, you will observe that I am currently running a name-and-shame campaign directed at those TDs who voted in favour of the Land and Conveyancing Law Reform Act 2013, aka the Eviction Bill. Given the fatal consequence to families and devastation caused to children, I expect you were not informed of the ramifications of such a bill when you voted in its favour July 2013.

In light of your public stance I respectfully ask in the name of suicide victims, their families, relatives and friends and the tens of thousands of families tonight who live in fear of eviction, that you publicly revoke your support for the Land and Conveyancing Law Reform Act 2013.

To save so many lives will take but one sentence from you. I hope and pray you hold the courage to show this nation's people there is at least one politician in Ireland who puts his country before his pride.

Tom Darcy.

In conclusion, not one TD has acknowledged or apologised to the Irish people for signing the Land and Conveyancing Law Reform Bill 2013. Regardless of the number of children who have watched their families being thrown out onto the street, the tens of thousands of families under direct threat of eviction and individuals who have taken their own lives, our public representatives remain silent.

APPENDIX B

Bonfire of the Vanities and the Evidence?

If even a fraction of the lurid rumours surrounding the imminent collapse of the trial in Dublin, of Seán FitzPatrick, the former chairman of Anglo Irish Bank and the poster boy of the Celtic Tiger era, turn out to be true, then the system of corporate oversight and regulation and the system of justice in Ireland are in one helluva mess. That such rumours (and at this stage they are no more than that) – including a bonfire of the evidence, a key witness having checked into a mental hospital or otherwise disappeared, the alteration of witness statements – are even circulating with a degree of credibility should be sounding alarm bells across the Irish State. What is even more alarming are suggestions circulating in the financial intelligence community that the Irish State has been playing for time in recent months in order to come up with a version of events that does not sound like the script for a sequel to *The Godfather Part III*.

Mr FitzPatrick has become the symbol of all that was wrong in Ireland at the height of the bubble economy, if such economies have high points. Anglo Irish Bank, grew out of the postwar demand of the Irish people for tea – then trading as Tea Importers Ltd – and morphed over the years into the hubristic entity that it became. It is seen by Irish people, and especially those in business, as emblematic of all that was wrong: political cosiness with the governments of the time, a lack of any real understanding of the international markets in which the bank was dabbling, a lack of adherence to even the most minimal ethical standards, an overwhelming ambition, and, if the bulk of the Irish people are to be believed, outright criminality and fraud at the heart of the enterprise for the entire period. Throw into the mix Minister for Finance who did not have a bank account; brown envelopes stuffed with money; dig-outs for senior politicians whose salaries for their posts, in what is essentially a county council, were larger than those in almost any other state in the EU and the developed world – and you have the toxic mix that has led to a complete collapse in trust in the system of law and regulation in the country.

If the rumours are not true then, of course, Mr FitzPatrick has been done a grave injustice. He is, as is anyone else, entitled to a fair trial. A prosecution starts the moment a person is investigated, and the rule of law which supposedly obtains in Ireland requires that the investigation process, the decision to prosecute and the trial itself are conducted in accordance with a few basic rules. These include the presumption of innocence, impartiality of the prosecutor and a fundamental commitment to fairness and justice. However, if the rumours are true, then not only were the norms of financial integrity lacking in Ireland but also an understanding of those basic concepts critical to the functioning of a modern democracy.

Any announcement (and we are led to believe that one is imminent) that the trial of Mr FitzPatrick has collapsed will lead to outrage amongst those in Ireland struggling to cope with the consequences of the self-induced collapse of the Irish banks over five years ago. Most people will not believe the reasons the State gives, no matter how much evidence supports the public version. The people of Ireland are so mistrustful of their system of justice and of politicians, lawyers and judges generally that they will believe the most lurid of explanations in circulation or to theories of conspiracies involving even more and larger brown envelopes. And there lies the rub for Ireland. If its own people are so mistrustful of the governance of the country and of the system of regulation and justice, how do others outside perceive the country's standing? Most in the international financial markets will be scratching their heads, and those at the core of the belated regulation of the financial markets will be reprogramming their risk models to take account of what is a visibly failing system if not a state. The swarms of people in Ireland whose mortgages are now in the hands of unregulated vulture companies and who are facing possession of their homes in vast numbers will not take this one lying down.

Commentators have observed how the Irish people have responded to the crisis visited upon them by their leaders with dignity and commitment to recovery and have not opted for the street protest, or at least not for the violent kind. Faced with yet another example of what will be seen as the operation of a self-interested clique protecting its own and preventing the truth ever emerging, that reticence may finally evaporate. It is already the case that the courts and judges are rightly or wrongly vilified. They are seen as mouthpieces for the banks, vulture companies and the politicians seeking to shore up the stage set of an economic 'recovery' based on a repetition of previous mistakes. While the Government trumpets a 'recovery', predicted, it would appear, on the fact that house prices are rising again in certain areas, the courts are handing out possession orders by the sackful based on the flimsiest of legal procedures. The vulture funds, meanwhile, are selling the same distressed assets over the heads of families struggling to keep their homes together and then there are those being forced to borrow at, once again, unsustainable levels. That scenario in a country with a history of absentee landowners visiting ruin on the Irish people does not play well. And it is hardly surprising that the resulting grassroots activism has echoes of the latter part of the nineteenth century. In reality, the picture, including the appearance and function of the institutions of justice, such as the Four Courts in Dublin, is once more reminiscent of a period of laissez-faire capitalism than of a modern European state with a commitment to the welfare of its people, openness and justice.

If this is not a wake-up call for Ireland and its system of oversight, regulation and justice, then it may end up as a funeral march for the entire system. Ireland is already largely beholden to the EU and, like a schoolchild that has been grounded, is required to seek the approval of its parents in Germany and elsewhere for any significant move. If, even in that scenario, it cannot manage its own affairs with anything like a semblance of order, then there is little hope for a future or for the emergence of an economy that can allow the long-suffering people of the country to believe in stability and an equal share in the future.

The above comments are the opinions of a British senior counsel. The senior counsel is a lawyer specialising in banking law and the law of financial markets, derivatives and securitisation. Based in Berlin, he has regular dealings with Irish clients. He has written extensively on the financial crisis from a legal and historical perspective.

12 May 2015

APPENDIX C

Note to Our American Cousins

I suspect that many Americans lost millions of dollars in the stock markets as a result of being sold questionable financial products by Irish banks. As this book goes to print, another revelation has been exposed in the Irish banking enquiry. Richie Boucher, CEO of Bank of Ireland, has admitted that his balance sheets are totally fictional. It is no wonder that Bank of Ireland delisted from the New York Stock Exchange in 2015 (which had cost €10 million to join), the intention being to distance themselves from the watchful eye of the Securities and Exchange Commission (SEC). Furthermore, it appears that in an effort to avoid accountability and prosecution from those it had conned out of their savings, the Irish Government introduced the Companies Act 2014, which removed the charter of the Governor and Company of the Bank of Ireland.

To our friends and family in the United States of America, whose nostalgic belief in this country of saints and scholars has now been replaced by corrupt bankers and liars, you can end this brutality that befalls your Irish cousins should your judiciary not be politically driven or appointed and your judges not indebted to Irish banks. Richie Boucher admitted that the Bank of Ireland, like all Irish banks, has falsified their balance sheets, and our own bond-holding Minister for Finance, Michael Noonan, acknowledged that our banks had no banking licence. Furthermore, our Irish police force ignores criminal allegations against Irish banks. Your General Attorney, with little effort, could bring these corrupt bankers to face federal charges of wire fraud, share fixing and other criminal offenses. It would just take a few American citizens to break the chains of corruption.

Our ancestors and your grandparents helped to create America; you can now help create a better Ireland by seeking for justice to be done. Stop the atrocity against innocent Irish women and children. Please initiate legal proceedings against Irish banks who traded illegally in America and stole from you, lied to you and conned the people of the Irish Nation.

APPENDIX D

Statement to An Garda Síochána

I Thomas Darcy aged eighteen years and older of 21 Myra Manor Kinsealy Make this Statement of facts upon which I believe to be the truth.

I state the Allied Irish Banks PLC as registered in the companies office of Ireland and holding themselves as conducting or being willing to conduct the business of banking in the Irish state subject to the statute law and regulations imposed by Central Bank of Ireland Acts of 1941-1989 and Company laws of 1963-2010 and the laws of this Irish State operated a Financial Institution for the periods between 2006-2007-2008-2009 in contravention of the said laws.

I state the Allied Irish Banks operated in the securitisation of loans contrary to the laws of this state and Europe.

I state the Allied Irish Banks operated without a perfected Banking Licence in contravention of the Central Bank Acts of 1941-1989 and further state the Allied Irish Banks PLC on renewal of its legislated Annual Banking Licence with intent materially concealed and dishonestly omitted facts by false and misrepresentation in which to obtain said Banking licence.

I state the Allied Irish Banks PLC. Contravened its legislated obligation to deposit securities to the Central Bank of Ireland in respect to its loan to deposit ratios and liquidity ratios under the Central Bank Acts of 1941-1989 on renewal of its Banking licence in accordance with statute law. I state the Allied Irish Banks PLC with intent criminally ignored its mandatory obligation to inform the Central Bank of Ireland of material facts and changes to its status and exposure as a Financial Institution as set forth in the Central Bank Acts of 1941-1989.

I state the Allied Irish Banks traded as a financial institution in contravention to solvency requirements as prescribed by the statute of Ireland and as registered within the Companies office under the C1 mortgage title, declaring the said bank to be insolvent, dated the 15th of February 2008. I state the Allied Irish Banks with intent ignored its legal responsibility to inform its shareholders, account holders of its pledging of all of its assets to the IFSA and CBI.

I further state the Allied Irish Banks have engaged in such practices of Interest swap manipulation, default swap manipulation and false claim to legal and equitable rights to facilities now transferred.

I state the Allied Irish Banks pledged ALL its assets and securities, profits present and future to the financial services authority and the Central Bank of Ireland on the 15th of February 2008 under contract, I say this was not reflected in the banks' financial records, contrary to law. Furthermore I say the said contract crystallised on the 25th of September of 2008 on the actions of the Allied Irish Banks seeking state guarantee.

I say and believe the omission of the aforementioned legislated securities and material changes were not reflected in the annual financial records presented to the Companies office in December 2008 reflecting such exposures and true financial status, I say the accounts of 2006-2007-2008-2009 by the Allied Irish Banks PLC do not reflect the insolvency of the Banks.

I state the Allied Irish Banks PLC with intent contravened Company Law of the Irish State by omitting and concealing its mandatory obligations to produce a True annual financial reflection of its status. I state the Allied Irish Banks PLC contravened its Memorandum and Articles of Association under Company law and statute law by issuing a false and misleading set of financial records to its shareholders for the periods of 2006-2007-2008-2009. I state the Allied Irish Banks PLC was required by statute law to inform its shareholders of all material changes and exposures to the status of the company as required by law and with intent failed to do so. I seek An Garda Síochána to enforce the laws of this country as set forth in our enacted Constitution dated the 1st of July 1937 and bring criminal charges against the Allied Irish Banks PLC, its Directors and agents for the breaches and violations of the laws of this state.

APPENDIX E

C1 Mortgage Registration Form

Particulars of a charge created by a company incorporated in the State
Section 99, Companies Act, 1963, as amended

Certificate that the charge was presented for registration in the country where the property is situate
Section 99(5), Companies Act, 1963

Companies Re

3314652

CN:

Companies Acts, 1963 to 2001

Company Number
| 2 | 2 | 0 | 4 | 5 |

C1

Please complete in black typescript or in BOLD CAPITALS, referring to explanatory notes

Company name
in full Anglo Irish Bank Corporation Public Limited Company

Description of the Charge *note two*
(a) ☐   (b) ☐   (c) ☐   (d) ☐   (e) ☐   (f) ☒   (g) ☐   (h) ☐   (i) ☐

Date created
| Day | Month | Year |
| 1 5 | 0 2 | 2 0 0 8 |

Amount secured *note one*
☐ All monies and/or obligations which now are, or at any time may become, due or owing to the security holder by the company on any account and all other liabilities whatsoever of the company to the security holder whether actual or contingent and whether as principal debtor, guarantor, surety or otherwise.

☒ All monies and/or obligations which now are, or at any time may become, due or owing to the security holder under an agreement between

| The Central Bank and Financial Services Authority of Ireland |
| And |
| The Company |

Certified to be a true copy/extract of a document filed with the Registrar on _12|06_
day of _2008_
Dated this _02_ of _07 | 2013_
Signed _Sarah Clare_
An Officer duly authorised pursuant to the Companies Acts 1963-2012

| Dated | Day | Month | Year |
| | 1 5 | 0 2 | 2 0 0 8 |

☐ Amount € _____   Plus interest and charges YES/NO *delete as appropriate*

☐ Other *please specify*

Certificate to be completed regarding property outside the State *note three*

X It is not necessary, to register the charge in any other country to make it valid or effectual.

☐ It is necessary to register the charge in another country to make it valid or effectual,

| | Day | Month | Year |

and the charge was presented for registration on

at

or

☐ A separate form, 47C, shall be delivered in due course to the registrar with the appropriate fee.

Presenter details
Name	Eugene F. Collins
Address	Temple Chambers, 3 Burlington Road,
	Dublin 4.
DX number	25
Telephone number	2026400
Email	dekelly@efc.ie

DX Exchange	Dublin
Fax Number	6675200
Reference Number	EG/dek/a22846.91

187

Appendix C

Persons entitled to the charge
note four

Name	Central Bank and Financial Services Authority of Ireland
Address	PO Box 559, Dame Street, Dublin 2.
Name	
Address	
Name	
Address	
Name	
Address	
Name	
Address	

Short particulars of the property charged
note five

The Company, as legal and beneficial owner and subject to Clause 4 of the Deed of Charge, as a continuing security for the discharge and payment of the Secured Obligations, thereby charged by way of first floating charge to the Bank all its right, title, interest and benefit, present and future, in and to each of the Eligible Securities from time to time (the "Secured Assets").

Where:

"Secured Obligations" means all present and future liabilities whatsoever of the Company to the Bank or to the European Central Bank or the national central bank of a Member State that has adopted the euro in respect of its participation in TARGET2 – Ireland which become due, owing or payable by the Company to the Bank and/or such other party under or in respect of, and subject to the terms and conditions of, the Deed of Charge and the Terms and Conditions including, without limitation, all obligations of the Company to an AL NCB under an AL Agreement entered into pursuant to (and as defined in) the Terms and Conditions and all other obligations and liabilities of the Company from time to time arising under the Deed of Charge.

Negative Pledge included.

Defined terms have the meaning assigned to them in the Annex hereto.

☒ Further particulars *note six*

Verification
note seven

Either side or both sides to the transaction (or their solicitors) may sign. If only one party signs then a certified copy of the deed creating the charge should be enclosed. The notes following constitute part of this form.

Signature of applicant	Position held
Eileen Grace, Eugene F Collins	Partner
Name *in block letters or typed*	Nature of interest in the charge
EILEEN GRACE,	Solicitor for the Company
Counter-signed	Position held
	Solicitor for the Company
Name *in block letters or typed*	Nature of interest in the charge
EILEEN GRACE	Company

☒ Place an X in the box if the deed is attached.

CRO AN OIFIG UM CHLÁRÚ CUIDEACHTAÍ / COMPANIES REGISTRATION OFFICE

(a)   where the participant no longer meets the access criteria laid down in Article 4 or the requirements laid down in Article 8(1)(a)(i) of Annex 1 to the Terms and Conditions;

(b)   the opening of insolvency proceedings in relation to the participant;

(c)   the submission of an application relating to the proceedings referred to in subparagraph (b);

(d)   the issue by the participant of a written declaration of its inability to pay all or any part of its debts or to meet its obligations arising in relation to intraday credit;

(e)   the entry of the participant into a voluntary general agreement or arrangement with its creditors;

(f)   where the participant is, or is deemed by the Bank to be, insolvent or unable to pay its debts;

(g)   where the participant's credit balance on its PM account or all or a substantial part of the participant's assets are subject to a freezing order, attachment, seizure or any other procedure that is intended to protect the public interest or the rights of the participant's creditors;

(h)   where participation of the participant in another TARGET2 component system and/or in an ancillary system has been suspended or terminated;

(i)   where any material representations or pre-contractual statement made by the participant under the applicable law is incorrect or untrue; or

(j)   the assignment of all or a substantial part of the participant's assets;

"Participating NCB's" means the national central banks of the European Union Member States which have adopted the single currency in accordance with the Treaty establishing the European Community;

"Receiver" means a receiver appointed under the Deed of Charge or pursuant to statutory powers by the Bank upon the Security becoming enforceable and includes more than one such receiver and substituted receiver.

"Secured Obligations" means all present and future liabilities whatsoever of the Company to the Bank or to the European Central Bank or the national central bank of a Member State that has adopted the euro in respect of its participation in TARGET2 – Ireland which become due, owing or payable by the Company to the Bank and/or such other party under or in respect of, and subject to the terms and conditions of, the Deed of Charge and the Terms and Conditions including, without limitation, all obligations of the Company to an AL NCB under an AL Agreement entered into pursuant to (and as defined in) the Terms and Conditions and all other obligations and liabilities of the Company from time to time arising under the Deed of Charge.

"Security" means the security from time to time constituted by or pursuant to the Deed of Charge and each and every part thereof;